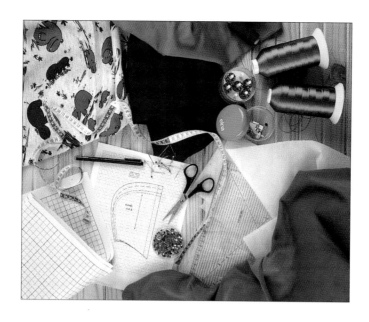

First published in the UK in 1995 by
New Holland (Publishers) Ltd
24 Nutford Place
London W1H 6DQ

ISBN 1 85368 540 2 (hbk)
ISBN 1 85368 605 0 (pbk)

Editor: Thea Coetzee
Designers: Suzanne Fortescue and Janice Evans
Cover design: Darren McLean
Design assistant: Lellyn Creamer
Photographer: Juan Espi
Stylist: Nancy V Richards
Colour illustrations: Jacques le Roux and Darren McLean
Line drawings: Jacques le Roux

Typesetting: Struik DTP
Reproduction: Unifoto (Pty) Ltd
Printing and binding: Tien Wah Press (Pte.) Ltd, Singapore

CONTENTS

INTRODUCTION

These days more and more people are doing their own sewing – not only as a hobby, but also as a way of saving money. For this, the overlocker is indispensable. I trust that this book will equip you with plenty of ideas for designing and making your own creations, and that in the process you and your overlocker will become inseparable friends.

Before buying an overlocker, it is important to determine exactly what your needs are. Visit at least three dealers, attending their demonstrations, in order to decide whether a particular overlocker fulfils all your needs. Pay special attention to the characteristics of that particular model, how it is threaded, the usage and availability of extra accessories, the guarantee and whether lessons are offered. After purchasing your overlocker, you must make a point of attending the lessons offered by the dealer as soon as possible.

ORGANIZING A SUITABLE SEWING AREA

Choose your sewing area carefully. Unfortunately it is not always possible to have a permanent sewing area, because extra space is often limited to the study or guest room. It is important, however, that there should be sufficient working surfaces, power points and light.

- *Working surfaces:* The sewing machine and overlocker must be easily accessible, preferably placed alongside each other on a solid surface. The machines should not vibrate when you are sewing. The working surface must also be of the correct height – approximately 71 cm (28 in) above the floor – and the chair must be suitable for this height. Position the machines in such a way that you can easily move from one to another, ensuring that no power cords are in the way.
- *Power points:* You will need power points for the sewing machine, overlocker, iron and lighting.
- *Light:* The room should preferably get plenty of sunlight. If there is not enough sunlight, artificial lighting must be installed. Fluorescent lights are economical and effective.

NEEDLES

Choose the correct needles when using your overlocker and sewing machine. Needle sizes 70, 80 and 90, depending on the make of your overlocker, can be used on an overlocker only. It is important to consult the instruction manual or your dealer, otherwise your overlocker could develop technical problems, such as skipping stitches.

TYPES OF NEEDLES

- Universal needles are suitable for woven fabrics, such as polyester, cotton, twill or calico. These needles can be used on the overlocker as well as the sewing machine.
- Ballpoint needles are suitable for thin woven or knitted fabrics and silky fabrics such as polyester cotton. As the rounded point of the needle enters between the fibres, it will not damage the fibres or make holes in the fabric. These needles can be used on the overlocker as well as on the sewing machine.
- Stretch needles are suitable for stretch fabrics, such as T-shirting and tracksuiting. They can be used on the overlocker as well as on the sewing machine.
- Twin needles are used for top stitching on tracksuits and casual wear. Twin needles are available in widths of 2.5 mm (⅛ in) and 4 mm (¼ in) – the distance between the two needles. The 4 mm (¼ in) twin needle is most often used for top stitching on stretch fabrics. The twin needle is available in sizes 75 and 90 and can only be used on the sewing machine. It is easy to recognize the twin needle suitable for use on stretch fabrics: either the needle shaft or the needle itself is blue.

NOTE: Neither denim needles nor leather needles can be used on an overlocker, as these needles are shaped in such a way that they will hit against the loopers when sewing.

USING NEEDLES ON THE OVERLOCKER

- Always use two needles of the same type on the overlocker, for example two ballpoint needles.
- Always use two needles of the same size on the overlocker, for example two size 80 needles.

NOTE: Whenever one needle breaks, replace both needles. This will ensure that you are always using two needles of the same type and size.

- When replacing a needle, ensure that the flat side of the needle faces the back of the overlocker and the round side faces the front.
- When replacing a needle, be sure to push the needle up as high as possible before tightening the needle clamp screw with a screwdriver or an Allen key.

- Change the needles regularly to ensure trouble-free sewing – after every four to six hours of sewing.
- On a four-thread safety stitch overlocker, the right needle is always situated slightly lower than the left needle. If both needles are positioned at the same height, the timing of the needles will be inaccurate in relation to the loopers and the overlocker will skip stitches.
- On a four- or five-thread overlocker with a chain stitch, the front needle is always situated slightly lower than the back needle. If both are positioned at the same height, the overlocker will skip stitches.

THREADS

- Overlocking threads are available in reels of 1 000 m (1 100 yd) and 5 000 m (5 500 yd). Do not use smaller reels than these, as doing so will affect the tension.
- Polyester cotton thread consists of a cotton-wrapped polyester strand and can be used on the needles as well as on the loopers. The cotton sheath ensures a soft thread, whilst the polyester core provides strength and elasticity. Polyester cotton thread is well suited for use on the overlocker because, as the machine sews at a speed of approximately 1 300 – 1 500 stitches per minute, the thread must be able to stretch, irrespective of the type of fabric used.
- Floss (bulk nylon) can only be used on the loopers of an overlocker. It consists of polyester and nylon fibres and produces softer, stronger seams with more elasticity.
- Decorative threads for the overlocker include metallic thread, ribbon thread, top stitching and buttonhole threads, embroidery thread, crochet thread and even wool. Crochet or embroidery thread (no. 8 or 12) or industrial wool can be used on the overlocker.
- Decorative threads can be used on the needles as well as on the loopers, provided that the thread is thin enough to go through the eye of the needle or looper. The thicker the thread, the lower must be the tension setting. For crochet thread,

for example, the tension setting will be 0, and for metallic thread it will be approximately 1–5.

As decorative threads normally do not stretch very much, the tension knob of the overlocker through which the thread runs must be set as low as possible, and you must sew as slowly as possible to prevent the thread from snapping.

As the type of decorative thread you will use depends on the type of fabric and the style of the garment you are making, it is a good idea to test it on a piece of scrap fabric before sewing your garment.

THREADING

Although all overlockers may look similar and operate in a similar way, there are slight differences in the way they are threaded. Consult your instruction manual or dealer for the specific order and finer details.

Although most instruction manuals recommend that new threads simply be knotted above the tension knobs and then pulled or stitched through, I strongly discourage it, for two good reasons. Firstly, doing this may damage the tension spring on the tension knob and, secondly, you will never really learn to thread your overlocker. After purchasing your overlocker, practise threading it a few times before you start making any articles or garments.

TENSION

Remember to keep the thread taut when threading your overlocker to ensure that the thread is properly inserted into the tension spring on the tension knob. If the thread is not properly inserted into the spring, the overlocking stitch will form loops, depending on which thread is not inserted. Therefore you

NOTE: When a 'balanced' tension is indicated for the overlocker, it simply means that the tension is at the normal setting. It also means that the loopers of the overlocker will form a stitch on the edge of the fabric.

should first make sure that the thread is inserted into the spring before adjusting the tension knob.

The tension settings on a four-thread overlocker are as follows:

LEFT NEEDLE

This is the outside needle. Of the four tension settings on your overlocker, the tension for this needle must always be the highest, because it controls the thread which holds the seam together and prevents the seam from pulling open.

RIGHT NEEDLE

This is the inside needle and is also known as the mock safety stitch. The tension setting for this needle must always be lower than that of the outside needle, as this controls the thread which supports the outside thread. If the tension is set too high, the seam will pucker.

UPPER LOOPER

The upper looper controls the thread which lies across on top of the stitching. The tension setting on this looper must always be as low as possible to prevent the seam from puckering or pulling open.

LOWER LOOPER

The lower looper controls the thread which lies across the bottom of the stitching. The tension setting on this looper must always be as low as possible to prevent the seam from puckering or pulling open.

NOTE: On an overlocker, 0 signifies a very low tension setting and 9 a very high setting.

STITCH LENGTH

This is the distance between the stitches and the loops formed. The desired stitch length will depend on the thickness of the fabric and the type of finish. Use short stitches on thin fabrics, such as silk or viscose, and for sewing a narrow hem. Use longer stitches for heavier or thicker fabrics, such as denim or wadding (batting), and for gathering.

PRESSURE KNOB

The pressure knob on the overlocker is used either to increase or to decrease the pressure of the sewing foot on the fabric. For thin fabrics, increase pressure (turn knob in), in order to prevent the fabric from slipping or puckering under the sewing foot. For thicker fabrics, decrease pressure (turn knob out) in order to prevent the fabric from bunching or getting stuck.

MOVING AND FIXED BLADES

There are two blades on the overlocker which will cut the edge of the fabric before it is overlocked.

The *moving blade* is the blade that can be disengaged when you want to do decorative sewing, if you don't want to cut the fabric.

The *fixed blade* controls the cutting width of the overlocker. This blade can be adjusted according to what type of fabric is used.

Depending on the make and model of your overlocker, one of these two blades must be replaced when it no longer cuts the edges of the fabric cleanly. Consult your dealer or instruction manual. It is advisable to replace the blade after approximately 6–12 months if you sew quite regularly or after 12–18 months if you do not sew that often.

DIFFERENTIAL FEED

Most overlockers are equipped with a differential feed for perfect fabric control. This means that the overlocker has two sets of 'feed dogs'. The purpose of the feed dog is to feed the fabric through from the bottom. The speed of the feed dog can be controlled by adjusting the differential feed knob.

When the differential feed knob is set on 0.5–0.7, the front feed dog feeds the fabric through at a slower speed than the back one, in order to prevent thin fabrics, such as silk, viscose or net, from puckering.

When the differential feed knob is set on 1.0, the front and back feed dogs feed the fabric through at exactly the same speed. This is the normal setting and is generally used when sewing cotton, polyester, linen or tracksuiting.

When the differential feed knob is set on 1.5, the front feed dog feeds the fabric through faster than the back feed dog. This setting is more suitable for thicker fabrics, such as double-knitted tracksuiting and thin knitting, and it can also be used when you are joining seams or sewing over seams, for example the underarm seams.

When the differential feed knob is set on 2.0, the front feed dog will feed the fabric through faster than it will at a setting of 1.5. This prevents knitted fabrics from waving or stretching and thick fabrics from bunching up. Use this setting when you are sewing very thick fabrics such as denim, knitted fabric or leather, and also when applying rib trim, sewing wadding, or covering shoulder pads with fabric. This setting can also be used to gather fabrics, as described under DECORATIVE FINISHES USING THE OVERLOCKER on pages 15–20.

OVERLOCKING STITCHES
The overlocking stitches described below are formed around a stitch tongue with the use of the needles and the loopers on the overlocker. The type of stitching that results will depend on the number of needles and loopers that are used.

In this book instructions are given only for the four-thread overlocker under each project. If you have a three-thread overlocker, you have no choice regarding the width of the decorative stitchings, and your seams will always be sewn with a three-thread overlocking stitch. If, however, you have a five-thread overlocker, you can decide on the width of the decorative stitchings, either by using plates for obtaining different widths, or by adjusting the needles. If you have the above-mentioned options on your particular overlocker, your seams can be sewn with a three-, four- or five-thread overlocking stitch.

ACCESSORIES
It is a good idea to consult your dealer or agent for more information regarding the different accessories, feet and attachments which are available for your particular make and model of overlocker.

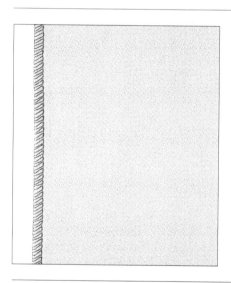

THREE-THREAD OVERLOCKING
This overlocking stitch is formed around the stitch tongue with the use of one needle and two loopers. This is the most basic stitch formed on an overlocker. This stitch can be used on its own if, for example, it is used for a seam that is not under stress. It can also be used in conjunction with a sewing machine to finish an edge. All decorative finishing, for example flatlocking and pin-tucks (see pages 15–20), is always done with three threads.

NEEDLE	THREAD	TENSION
Right needle	polyester cotton thread	4–8 (balanced)
Upper looper	polyester cotton thread	1–5 (balanced)
	floss	0–2 (balanced)
Lower looper	polyester cotton thread	1–5 (balanced)
	floss	0–2 (balanced)

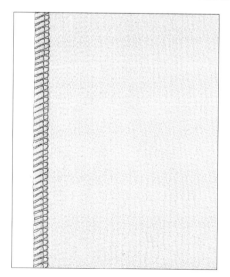

FOUR-THREAD OVERLOCKING
This stitch is formed around the stitch tongue with two needles and two loopers. This stitch is about 6–7 mm (about ¼ in) wide and is used for joining and overlocking seams. It is suitable for stretch fabrics as well as non-stretch fabrics. The overlocker can also be converted to sew a three-thread stitch by removing the left needle to form a narrow three-thread stitch, or by removing the right needle to form a wide three-thread stitch.

NEEDLE	THREAD	TENSION
Left needle	polyester cotton thread	4–8 (balanced)
Right needle	polyester cotton thread	3–6 (balanced)
Upper looper	polyester cotton thread	1–5 (balanced)
	floss	0–2 (balanced)
Lower looper	polyester cotton thread	1–5 (balanced)
	floss	0–2 (balanced)

FIVE-THREAD OVERLOCKING

The five-thread overlocker operates with two needles and three loopers.

Some models can also be used as a four-thread overlocker by changing the needles, or by inserting a special double needle suitable for sewing stretch fabrics. It also forms a two-thread chain stitch which functions as a conventional straight stitch and is mainly used for decorative purposes. Five-thread overlocking is most suitable for non-stretch fabrics.

NEEDLE	THREAD	TENSION
Chain needle	polyester cotton thread	2–5 (balanced)
Overlock needle	polyester cotton thread	3–6 (balanced)
Upper looper	polyester cotton thread	1–5 (balanced)
	floss	0–2 (balanced)
Lower looper	polyester cotton thread	1–5 (balanced)
	floss	0–2 (balanced)

The chain looper has a standard setting, depending on the make and model of the overlocker, and is not normally adjusted.

ACCESSORIES

TAPE GUIDE ATTACHMENT

This is an optional accessory which fits onto a three-, four or five-thread overlocker. It can be used on its own or in conjunction with the piping foot. It folds the pre-cut tape over, at the same time sewing it in between two layers of fabric. If used with the piping foot, nylon cord can be fed through the tape guide so that piping can be made and sewn onto the fabric in one operation.

1. Attach the tape guide attachment to the overlocker.

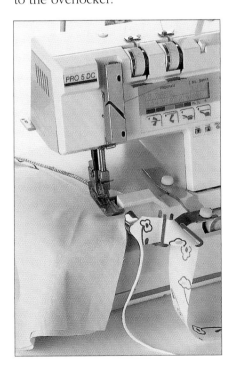

2. Feed 2.5 cm-wide (1 in-wide) pre-cut strips of fabric through the tape guide and under the foot.

3. Place one layer of fabric underneath and the other layer of fabric on top of the tape guide attachment and underneath the sewing foot or the piping foot.

4. Sew on the tape between the two layers of fabric using three-thread overlocking. With a four-thread overlocker, the left or right needle can be used, depending on the make and model of your overlocker.

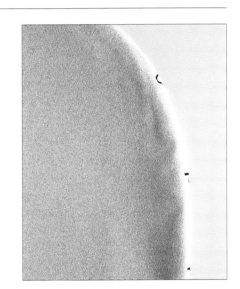

NEEDLE	THREAD	TENSION
Left/right needle	polyester cotton thread	4–8 (balanced)
Upper looper	polyester cotton thread	1–5 (balanced)
	floss	0–2 (balanced)
Lower looper	polyester cotton thread	1–5 (balanced)
	floss	0–2 (balanced)

Stitch length: 2½–3½
Differential feed: Depends on the thickness of the fabric and the number of layers
• The moving blade must be in the cutting position.

PIPING FOOT

The piping foot is always used in conjunction with the tape guide attachment on the overlocker. Use this foot to make your own piping and sew it onto fabric in one operation. The piping foot can be fitted onto a three-, four- or five-thread overlocker. With a four-thread over-locker, the left or right needle can be used, depending on the make and model of your overlocker.

1. Attach the piping foot onto your overlocker and use it in conjunction with the tape guide attachment to attach piping (see TAPE GUIDE ATTACHMENT above).

BIAS BINDER WITH CHAIN STITCH

1. The bias binder is optional and can only be fitted onto a five-thread overlocker. Cut bias strips of fabric (see page 11). Attach bias binder to the overlocker and feed bias strips of fabric through the bias binder and underneath the sewing foot.

NEEDLE	THREAD	TENSION
Chain needle	polyester cotton thread	2–5 (balanced)
Chain looper	polyester cotton thread	standard setting

Stitch length: 4–5
Differential feed: Depends on the thickness of the fabric
• The moving blade must be disengaged.

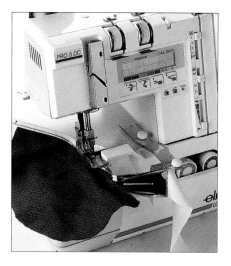

2. Place the fabric in the bias binder, ensuring that the edge of the fabric is encased in the bias strip. Adjust the bias binder so that the chain stitching is sewn onto the folded edge of the bias binding.

CHAIN FOOT

The chain foot is optional and can only be fitted onto a five-thread overlocker. This foot is used only when using a chain stitch as decorative top stitching. For method, see CHAIN STITCH WITH DECORATIVE THREAD, page 18.

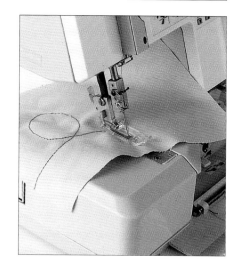

GATHERING ATTACHMENT OR FOOT

The gathering attachment or foot is an optional accessory which fits onto any three-, four- or five-thread overlocker. This attachment or foot enables you to gather the fabric on the bottom while at the same time sewing it onto the fabric on top.

The length of the fabric to be gathered should be approximately 1½–2 times the length of the fabric to which it is to be gathered. The number of gathers on the fabric will depend on the thickness of the fabric which is to be gathered. If the gathering attachment or foot is used in conjunction with the differential feed, the fabric will have more gathers. Either fabric or lace may be gathered in this way.

1. Attach the gathering foot or attachment onto the overlocker.

2. Place the fabric which is to be gathered underneath the gathering foot or attachment, with the right side up. Place the top layer of fabric, right side down, on top of the bottom layer of fabric.

3. When sewing, hold the top layer of fabric back slightly, while at the same time feeding the bottom layer of fabric into the machine.

4. The number of gathers on the fabric will depend on the thickness of the fabric, and the extent to which the top layer of fabric is being held back. Gathering can be done with either three- or four-thread overlocking.

NOTE: Consult your dealer about the use of accessories for your specific make and model of overlocker.

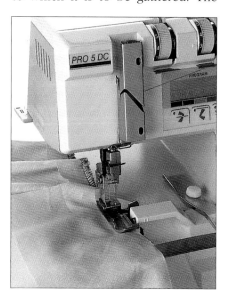

NEEDLE	THREAD	TENSION
Left needle	polyester cotton thread	4–8 (balanced)
Right needle	polyester cotton thread	3–6 (balanced)
Upper looper	polyester cotton thread	1–5 (balanced)
	floss	0–2 (balanced)
Lower looper	polyester cotton thread	1–5 (balanced)
	floss	0–2 (balanced)

Stitch length: 3–5
Differential feed: 1.5 for thin fabric, 2.0 for thick fabric
• The moving blade must be in the cutting position.

SEWING TECHNIQUES

TO MAKE BIAS BINDING

1. Cut a rectangle of fabric measuring 70 cm x 35 cm (27½ in x 13¾ in). This should be sufficient for a bias strip of approximately 3 m (3¼ yd). Fold one corner of the fabric to a 45° angle and draw a line on the fold, using a marking pen (Fig. 1).

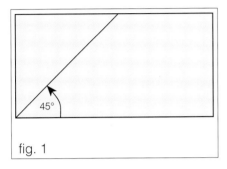

fig. 1

2. Draw lines parallel to the first line, 4 cm (1½ in) (or desired width) apart, until the far corner is reached.

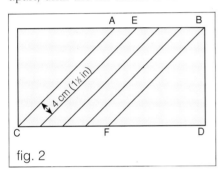

fig. 2

3. Mark the lines A to F, as shown on the diagram (Fig. 2). Cut out the parallelogram as shown (Fig. 3).

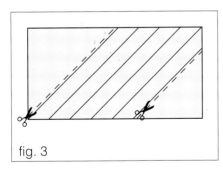

fig. 3

4. Take corner C to point E. Turn the fabric so that the raw edges are together and the lines form a V 1 cm (⅜ in) from the raw edge. Pin.

5. Bring corner B to point F (raw edges together) so that lines form a V 1 cm (⅜ in) from raw edge. Pin.

6. Using the sewing machine and straight stitch, sew 1 cm (⅜ in) from the raw edge on the pinned Vs (Fig. 4). Press the seam.

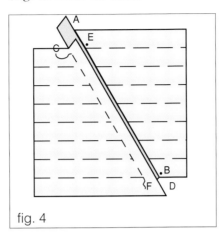

fig. 4

7. Starting at one uneven end, cut along the marked lines to form one continuous bias strip.

HOW TO MAKE PIPING WITH THE SEWING MACHINE

Insert nylon cord into the wrong side of a cut bias strip. Sew on right side, as close as possible to the cord, using the zipper foot on the sewing machine (Fig. 5). Make enough piping to suit your purpose.

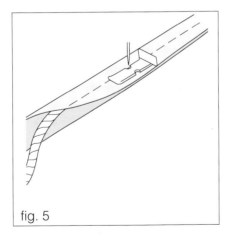

fig. 5

HOW TO ATTACH PIPING WITH THE SEWING MACHINE

Attaching piping to a corner

1. Pin piping to the RS of the fabric, 1 cm (⅜ in) from the edge.

2. Sew piping to fabric, ending about 5 cm (2 in) from the corner (Fig. 6a).

3. Lay the piping into position as far as the corner and pin. Clip the piping right up to the stitching, about 1 cm (⅜ in) from the edge of the fabric (Fig. 6a).

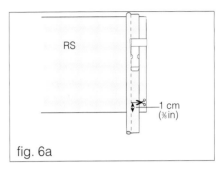

fig. 6a

4. Pin the piping so that it forms a corner 1 cm (⅜ in) from the edge (Fig. 6b). Sew piping to the fabric.

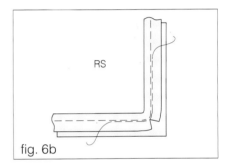

fig. 6b

Attaching piping on a curve

1. Pin piping to the RS of the fabric, 1 cm (⅜ in) from the edge. Sew the piping to the fabric, ending about 5 cm (2 in) from the curve.

2. Clip piping around curve so that it lies flat. Pin into position 1 cm (⅜ in) from edge of fabric (Fig. 7).

3. Sew the piping to the fabric.

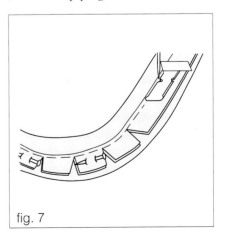

fig. 7

QUARTER PIN MARKING

Waist, sleeves and ankles
This technique is used throughout the book to pin elastic, rib trim and fabric in quarters:

Elastic or rib trim: Fold the elastic or rib trim in half on the seam, and mark the opposite half of the elastic or rib trim with a pin. Open out the elastic or rib trim and position the seam on the pin mark; mark both the resulting folds with pins. The elastic or rib trim is now divided into quarters (Fig. 8).

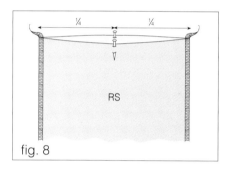

fig. 8

Fabric: The two side seams usually divide the fabric in half. If there is only one seam, fold the fabric in half on the seam and mark the opposite half of the fabric with a pin. If there are two side seams, place the two seams together; mark the centre front and centre back on the folds with pins. The fabric is now divided into quarters.

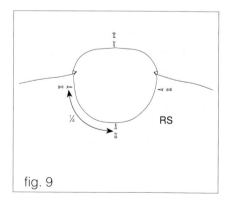

fig. 9

Round neck
Because the shoulder seams do not divide the round neck in half, a different method of quarter pin marking is applied here. Place the shoulder seams together and mark the centre front and the centre back on the folds with pins. Now place the centre front and centre back pins together and mark both the folds with pins (Fig. 9). The round neck is now divided into quarters.

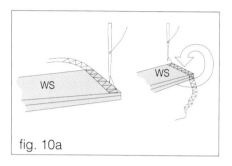

fig. 10a

JOINING ELASTIC TO FORM A CIRCLE
This technique is used to join elastic to form a circle so that it can be sewn to the waist, sleeves or ankles (Fig. 10a). It is also used for sewing up jerseys; to finish off the seam when the ribbing and jersey are knitted as one piece (in other words where there is no separate ribbing); and for children's clothes, where the sleeve and ankle openings are very small. The rib trim is attached first, before the underarm seam is sewn (Fig. 10b). Three- or four-thread overlocking can be used.

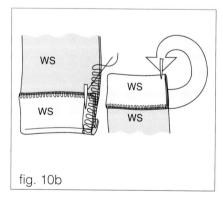

fig. 10b

1. With RS of the elastic or rib trim together, sew until you reach the end of elastic or rib trim, keeping elastic or rib trim next to the blade. The last stitch must be off the edge of the elastic or rib trim. When you stop sewing, ensure that the needle is above the elastic or rib trim.

2. Pull the needle thread(s) below the tension knob to loosen.

3. Release pressure foot, pull the stitches and thread off stitch tongue, remove elastic or rib trim from underneath foot and turn it around.

4. Now place the elastic or rib trim back underneath the pressure foot, keeping it next to the blade as before. Lower the foot, pull the needle thread(s) above the tension knob to tighten, and start sewing, making sure that the first stitch is on the elastic or rib trim.

5. Sew back on previous stitching, chaining off at the end.

6. If this technique is used to join elastic, there will be no loose threads on top of the elastic or at the end of the sleeve or waist of the jersey or top (Fig. 10).

ELASTICIZED BAND
1. This technique is normally used for finishing waist, sleeve and hood edges on tracksuit tops, and also for finishing waist and ankle edges on tracksuit bottoms (pants).

2. The elastic must be at least 2 cm (¾ in) wide.

3. **Join elastic** with three-thread over-locking **to form a circle** (Fig. 10).

4. Sew up the side seams of the garment to form a circle.

5. Place the elastic on the wrong side of the garment.

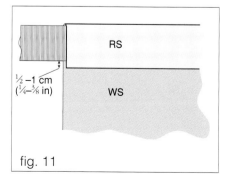

fig. 11

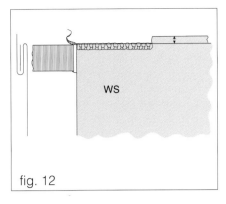

fig. 12

NEEDLE	THREAD	TENSION
Left needle	polyester cotton thread	4–8 (balanced)
Right needle	polyester cotton thread	3–6 (balanced)
Upper looper	polyester cotton thread	1–5 (balanced)
	floss	0–2 (balanced)
Lower looper	polyester cotton thread	1–5 (balanced)
	floss	0–2 (balanced)

Stitch length: 3–4
Differential feed: 1.5 or 2.0, depending on the thickness of the fabric
• The moving blade must be in the cutting position.

6. Fold edge of fabric to WS, covering the elastic, so that it extends ½–1 cm (¼–⅜ in) beyond elastic (Fig. 11).

7. Fold fabric back to the RS in line with the bottom edge of the elastic, making a fold in the fabric (Fig. 12).

8. Sew elastic to garment in a circle, using four-thread overlocking and keeping fold on top (Fig. 12).

SEWING IN A CIRCLE

Start approximately 2 cm (¾ in) from a seam. Begin to sew in a circle by sewing diagonally from the raw edge of the fabric to the stitching line. Continue sewing in a circle, always keeping the fabric in a straight line. When returning to the original starting point, sew over the diagonal stitches with which you started, so that the stitching is cut off, and then continue along the sewn edge for a further 2 cm (¾ in). Chain off and pull the looper threads tightly (Fig. 13). Cut the threads and apply stitch sealant to secure the ends (see page 23).

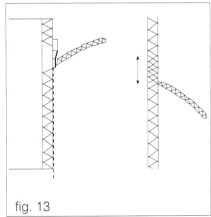

fig. 13

CURVED EDGES

Inside curve (Fig. 14a)
While sewing an inside curve, keep the fabric straight, in line with the edge of the plate. Sew very slowly, keeping your eye on the blade and not on the needle.

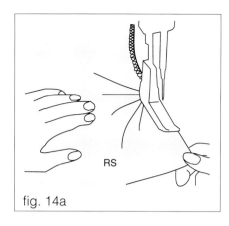

fig. 14a

Outside curve (Fig. 14b)

Keep fabric as straight as possible, in line with edge of the plate. Place your hand on the fabric, using your index finger to feed fabric through under pressure foot, while, at the same time, pulling it back with your remaining three fingers. Keep your eye on the blade, not on the needle.

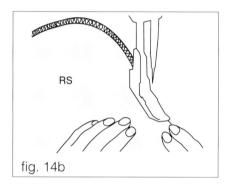

fig. 14b

CORNERS

Overlocking inside corners

1. This method is used when sewing pockets or slits. Clip the inside corner diagonally, the width of the stitching, 5–7 mm (about ¼ in).

2. Sew, keeping edge of fabric in line with edge of plate. Keep the fabric straight while sewing, pulling the clipped corner open (Fig. 15).

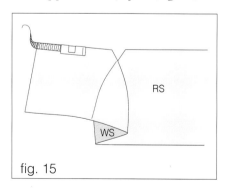

fig. 15

Turning at outside corners

1. Sew until you reach end of fabric, keeping edge of the fabric in line with the edge of the plate. When you stop sewing, make sure that the needle is above the fabric (Fig. 16a).

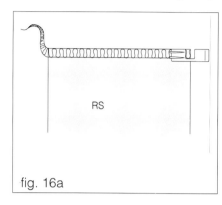

fig. 16a

2. Pull the needle thread (or needle threads) below the tension knob in order to loosen.

3. Release the pressure foot, pull the thread off the stitch tongue and turn the fabric 90 degrees (Fig. 16b).

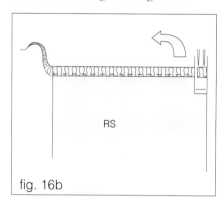

fig. 16b

4. Place the fabric back underneath the pressure foot, so that the first stitch that you sew will again be sewn on the fabric.

5. Before you start sewing, pull the needle thread (or needle threads) above the tension knob in order to tighten, and sew, keeping edge of fabric in line with edge of plate.

TO FINISH OFF SEAMS

Chaining off using stitch sealant (Fig. 17a)

End the stitching by sewing a chain of stitches off the edge of the fabric. Pull the looper threads tightly and then cut the chain off quite close to the stitching. Finally, apply a drop of stitch sealant to the thread ends and set aside for approximately one minute until completely dry.

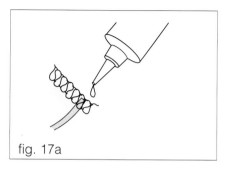

fig. 17a

Finishing by hand (Fig. 17b)

End the stitching by sewing a chain of stitches off the edge of the fabric. Undo the needle and looper threads and knot them together. Thread the threads through a large-eyed needle and sew back into the stitching for about 3–5 cm (1¼–2 in).

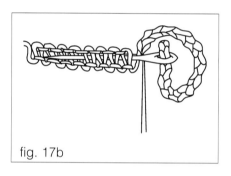

fig. 17b

UNPICKING

To undo three- or four-thread overlocking, cut and pull the needle threads. The overlocked edge will then come undone. Do not pull the looper threads if the needle threads happen to break (Fig. 18).

To undo flatlocking, cut the thread on the WS using a small pair of scissors or a stitch unpicker. Now undo the thread on the RS.

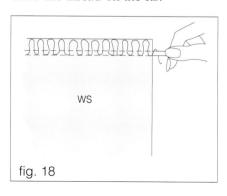

fig. 18

DECORATIVE FINISHES USING THE OVERLOCKER

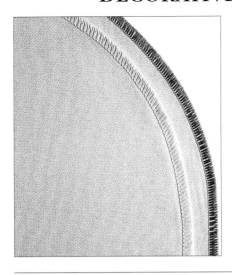

THREE-THREAD WIDE OVERLOCKING WITH FLOSS OR DECORATIVE THREAD

Always keep the right side of the fabric facing towards the top while sewing this stitch.

NEEDLE	THREAD	TENSION
Left needle	polyester cotton thread	4–8 (balanced)
Upper looper	floss	0–2 (balanced)
	decorative thread	0–5 (balanced)
Lower looper	floss	0–2 (balanced)
	decorative thread	0–5 (balanced)

Stitch length: 2–3½
Differential feed: Depends on the thickness of the fabric
• The moving blade must be in the cutting position.

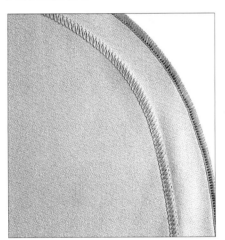

THREE-THREAD OVERLOCKING WITH FLOSS/DECORATIVE THREAD

Keep the right side of the fabric on top while sewing.

NEEDLE	THREAD	TENSION
Right needle	polyester cotton thread	4–8 (balanced)
Upper looper	floss	0–2 (balanced)
	decorative thread	0–5 (balanced)
Lower looper	floss	0–2 (balanced)
	decorative thread	0–5 (balanced)

Stitch length: 2–3½
Differential feed: Depends on the thickness of the fabric
• The moving blade must be in the cutting position.

THREE-THREAD WIDE PIN-TUCKS WITH FLOSS OR DECORATIVE THREAD

1. Draw several lines on the fabric or garment, approximately 4–5 cm (1½–2 in) apart.

2. Fold the fabric, with the wrong sides together, and sew.

3. Always keep the folded edge of the fabric precisely in line with the edge of the plate.

NOTE: If the tension of the upper looper is still too tight, even though it has been set on 0, and the stitches still do not lock on the edge of the fabric, it is also possible to loosen the tension by bypassing the lower threading point when you thread your overlocker.

NEEDLE	THREAD	TENSION
Left needle	polyester cotton thread	4–8 (balanced)
Upper looper	floss	0–2 (balanced)
	decorative thread	0–5 (balanced)
Lower looper	floss	0–2 (balanced)
	decorative thread	0–5 (balanced)

Stitch length: 2–3½
Differential feed: Depends on the thickness of the fabric
• The moving blade must be disengaged.

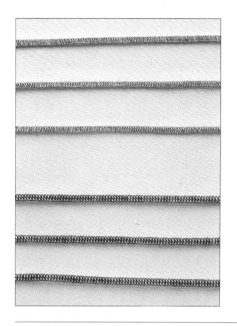

THREE-THREAD PIN-TUCKS WITH FLOSS OR DECORATIVE THREAD

1. Draw several lines on the fabric or garment, approximately 4–5 cm (1½–2 in) apart.

2. Fold the fabric, with the wrong sides together, and sew.

3. Always keep the folded edge of the fabric precisely in line with the edge of the plate.

NEEDLE	THREAD	TENSION
Right needle	polyester cotton thread	4–8 (balanced)
Upper looper	floss	0–2 (balanced)
	decorative thread	0–5 (balanced)
Lower looper	floss	0–2 (balanced)
	decorative thread	0–5 (balanced)

Stitch length: 2–3½
Differential feed: Depends on the thickness of the fabric
• The moving blade must be disengaged.

FLATLOCKING

Flatlocking is a seam which is sewn with three threads on two layers of fabric (or on one layer of fabric and one layer of lace). After sewing, the seam is pulled open in order to form a flat decorative seam on the right side of the fabric.

NOTE: The width of the decorative stitching depends on the size of the garment on which it is stitched and the extent to which the particular stitching must be emphasized.

• The width of the flatlocking depends on the width of the lace, the size of the strips or pieces of fabric to be joined, and the size of the article itself in relation to the decorative stitching. Depending on the width of the flatlocking you require, either the left needle or the right needle can be used together with both the loopers.

NOTE: If the tension of the upper looper is still too tight, even though it has been set on 0, and the stitches still do not lock on the edge of the fabric, loosen the tension by bypassing the lower threading point when you thread your overlocker.

• When sewing a flatlocked seam, the needle tension should be set lower while the tension on the lower looper is set higher.
• Flatlocking can be used to join lace onto an edge, or to sew it on top of the fabric. Use broderie anglaise, nylon or insertion lace which is wide enough to give an effective finish. When flatlocking fabric and lace together, always keep the lace at the bottom and the fabric on top.

NOTE: Always sew slowly when using decorative thread to prevent the thread from snapping or hooking, as this could damage your overlocker.

• A flatlocked seam can either be sewn on the raw edge of the fabric, or the fabric can be folded, so that the flatlocking is sewn in the centre of the fabric on a fold.
• When joining different colours of fabric, the flatlocking is always sewn on the raw edge of the fabric, and the moving blade should be in the cutting position.
• For a decorative flatlocked seam in the centre of the fabric, disengage the moving blade and keep the folded edge of the fabric precisely in line with the edge of the needle plate while sewing.

• When you are sewing a flatlocked seam, it is very important that the stitching should always face downwards or outwards when the seam is pulled open afterwards.
• For a decorative flatlocked finish on the right side of the fabric or garment, the wrong sides of the fabric are placed together.
• For a decorative ladder stitch on the right side of the fabric or garment, the right sides of the fabric are placed together.

Interesting effects can be obtained with the overlocker by using different types of thread for a flatlocked decoration. There is no need to keep to the rule of using the same type of thread or floss throughout.

NOTE: The stitch length and the differential feed setting will depend on the thickness of the fabric and the type of decorative thread or floss. (For a description of the various types of decorative threads available, see THREADS on page 6.) Only very basic guidelines are given for each of the decorative techniques. (For further guidelines regarding stitch length and differential feed, see STITCH LENGTH on page 7 and DIFFERENTIAL FEED on page 7.)

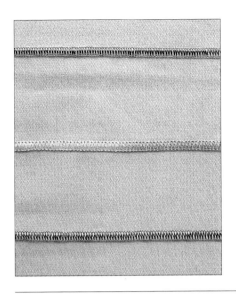

WIDE FLATLOCKING WITH FLOSS OR DECORATIVE THREAD

1. Always place the wrong sides of the fabric together.

2. After you have sewn the seam, it should be pulled open so that it forms flat decorative stitching on the right side of the fabric.

NEEDLE	THREAD	TENSION
Left needle	polyester cotton thread	0–2 (loosen)
Upper looper	floss	0–½ (loosen)
	decorative thread	0–1 (loosen)
Lower looper	polyester cotton thread	5–8 (tighten)
	floss	2–5 (tighten)

Stitch length: 2–3½
Differential feed: Depends on the thickness of the fabric
• The moving blade can be in the cutting position or disengaged.

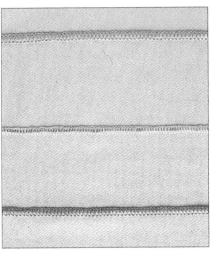

FLATLOCKING WITH FLOSS OR DECORATIVE THREAD

Place WS of the fabric together. Pull the seam open afterwards so that the stitching lies flat.

NEEDLE	THREAD	TENSION
Right needle	polyester cotton thread	0–2 (loosen)
Upper looper	floss	0–½ (loosen)
	decorative thread	0–1 (loosen)
Lower looper	polyester cotton thread	5–8 (tighten)
	floss	2–5 (tighten)

Stitch length: 2–3½
Differential feed: Depends on the thickness of the fabric
• The moving blade can be in the cutting position or disengaged.

WIDE FLATLOCKED LOOPS WITH FLOSS OR DECORATIVE THREAD

1. Draw several parallel lines on the fabric or garment.

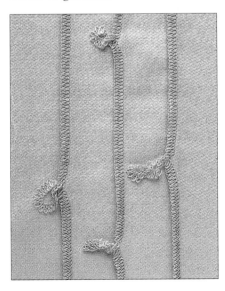

2. Fold the fabric on the lines you have drawn and keep the folded edge of the fabric in line with the edge of the needle plate.

3. Sew along the marked line for approximately 8–10 cm (3¼–4 in).

4. Tighten the needle tension to approximately 7–9.

5. Sew off edge of fabric for 5–6 cm (2–2¼ in), so that the stitches are formed around stitch tongue only.

6. Turn needle tension back to 4–6. Place the fabric back underneath the pressure foot and continue sewing for about 8–10 cm (3¼–4 in).

7. Repeat steps 4–6.

NEEDLE	THREAD	TENSION
Left needle	polyester cotton thread	4–6 (balanced)
Upper looper	floss	0–2 (balanced)
	decorative thread	0–5 (balanced)
Lower looper	polyester cotton thread	1–5 (balanced)
	floss	0–2 (balanced)

Stitch length: 2–3½
Differential feed: Depends on the thickness of the fabric
• The moving blade must be disengaged.

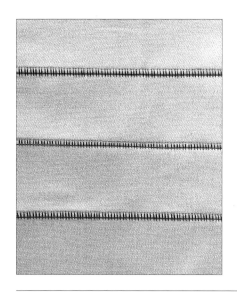

WIDE LADDER STITCH WITH FLOSS OR DECORATIVE THREAD

1. For ladder stitch, place the right sides of the fabric together.

2. After the seam has been sewn, it should be pulled open to form a flat decorative ladder stitch on the right side of the fabric.

NEEDLE	THREAD	TENSION
Left needle	decorative thread	0–2 (loosen)
Upper looper	polyester cotton thread	1–2 (loosen)
	floss	0–½ (loosen)
Lower looper	polyester cotton thread	5–8 (tighten)
	floss	2–5 (tighten)

Stitch length: 2–3½
Differential feed: Depends on the thickness of the fabric
• The moving blade can be in the cutting position or disengaged.

CHAIN STITCH WITH FLOSS OR DECORATIVE THREAD

This technique can only be used on a five-thread overlocker with a single chain stitch facility.

Depending on the desired effect, the right side or the wrong side of the stitching can be used on the outside of the garment. If you want to emphasize the straight stitching, use the decorative thread in the needle and the polyester cotton thread in the looper. If, however, you want to obtain a chain stitch loop effect, use decorative thread in the looper and the polyester cotton thread in the needle.

Use the chain stitch for sewing corners, circles and straight lines on the garment, or quilting a block.

Shirring elastic can also be used in the chain looper to gather sleeves, for instance, or for sewing any other decorative stitching.

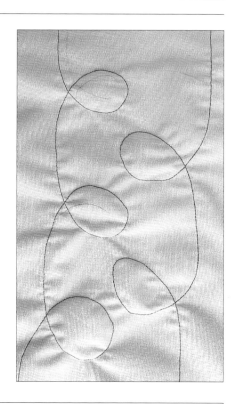

NOTE: On certain makes and models of five-thread over-locker, a sewing table or similar facility can be attached, which also enables you to sew straight stitching in the centre of the fabric, which is mainly decorative. It is a good idea to use the transparent chain stitch foot when sewing any form of decorative top stitching, so that it is easy for you to see where you are sewing.

NEEDLE	THREAD	TENSION
Chain needle	polyester cotton thread	2–5 (balanced)
	decorative thread	2–5 (balanced)
Chain looper	polyester cotton thread	standard setting
	floss	loosen tension knob
	decorative thread	loosen tension knob
	shirring elastic	loosen tension knob

Stitch length: 3–5
Differential feed: Depends on the thickness of the fabric
• The moving blade must be disengaged.
• Decrease the pressure on the pressure knob.

GATHERING WITH DIFFERENTIAL FEED

1. Fabric or lace can be gathered separately and sewn to the rest of the garment afterwards, or it can all be done in one operation.

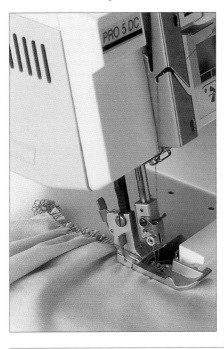

2. The more gathers you want on the fabric or lace, the tighter the needle tension must be. Cut the fabric at least 1½–2 times the required length when finished.

3. When gathering a single layer of fabric or lace, keep your index finger directly behind the pressure foot while sewing. This will assist in gathering the fabric.

4. When gathering fabric or lace and sewing it to the rest of the garment in one operation, place the fabric or lace to be gathered at the bottom, and the fabric to which it must be gathered on top, RS together.

5. Sew slowly, while holding the top layer back slightly and feeding the bottom fabric or lace through underneath the pressure foot.

6. The number of gathers depends on the thickness of the fabric or lace used and the extent to which the top layer of fabric is held back.

NEEDLE	THREAD	TENSION
Left needle	polyester cotton thread	5–9 (tighten)
Right needle	polyester cotton thread	5–8 (tighten)
Upper looper	polyester cotton thread	1–5 (balanced)
	floss	0–2 (balanced)
Lower looper	polyester cotton thread	1–5 (balanced)
	floss	0–2 (balanced)

Stitch length: 4–5
Differential feed: 1.5 for very thin fabrics, 2.0 for thicker fabrics
• The moving blade must be in the cutting position.

FLATLOCKED HEM WITH FLOSS OR DECORATIVE THREAD

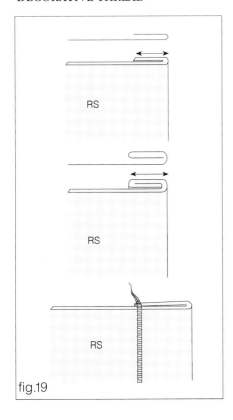

fig.19

1. Fold the fabric back to the wrong side to the desired hem width, then fold the fabric to the wrong side again so that the raw edge lies inside the fold. Always keeping the folded edge of the fabric in line with the edge of the plate, sew on the fold on the right side of the fabric through all the layers, thereby catching the raw edge of the fabric in the folded edge (Fig. 19).

2. The flatlocked hem should be pulled open after you have sewn it, so that the stitching lies flat and a flat hem is obtained.

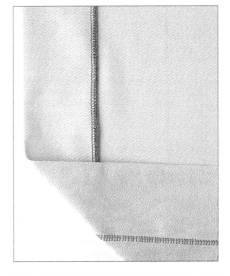

NEEDLE	THREAD	TENSION
Right needle	polyester cotton thread	0–2 (loosen)
Upper looper	floss	0–½ (loosen)
	decorative thread	0–1 (loosen)
Lower looper	polyester cotton thread	5–8 (tighten)
	floss	2–5 (tighten)

Stitch length: 2½–3½
Differential feed: Depends on the thickness of the fabric
• The moving blade must be disengaged.

WIDE FLATLOCKED HEM WITH FLOSS OR DECORATIVE THREAD

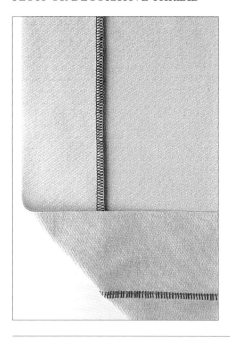

NOTE: Flatlocking can also be used to make a flat hem. Use the left needle for wide flatlocking and right needle for narrow flatlocking to ensure that the width of the hem is in proportion to the size of the article you are making. Disengage the moving blade before sewing a hem.

1. Fold fabric back to WS to desired hem width, then fold fabric again so that raw edge lies inside fold. Keeping folded edge in line with the edge of the plate, sew on RS of fabric on the fold through all layers, catching raw edge in folded edge.

2. Pull hem open afterwards so that a flat hem is obtained.

NEEDLE	THREAD	TENSION
Left needle	polyester cotton thread	0–2 (loosen)
Upper looper	floss	0–½ (loosen)
	decorative thread	0–1 (loosen)
Lower looper	polyester cotton thread	5–8 (tighten)
	floss	2–5 (tighten)

Stitch length: 2½–3½
Differential feed: Depends on the thickness of the fabric
• The moving blade must be disengaged.

PREPARING AND CUTTING OUT THE PATTERN

The patterns used in this book have been drawn onto graph paper and have all been reduced. Enlarge the patterns using a photocopier, or by drawing them onto graph paper. Remember that seam allowances have not been included, and that you have to add these yourself (as indicated on each pattern), unless otherwise mentioned.

NOTE: When you are scaling up a graph pattern, work very carefully, take extremely accurate measurements and make sure that the calculations are correct. This is extremely important, otherwise your garment will not fit you properly.

HOW TO SCALE UP A GRAPH PATTERN (Fig. 20)

1. First check scale to which pattern has been drawn. The scale in this book is 1 square = 1 cm² (⅜ in²), or 1 square = 2 cm² (¾ in²). This means that each square in the printed patterns represents 1 or 2 cm² (⅜ or ¾ in²) of squared paper. Draw a rectangle around the graph pattern which you

want to enlarge so that the pattern pieces fit into the space without extra rows of squares at the edges. Number the lines, starting from 0 (Fig. 20a).

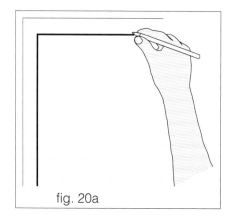

fig. 20a

2. Check scale of graph and mark off the same number of squares on graph paper. In this book 1 square = 1 cm² (⅜ in²), or 1 square = 2 cm² (¾ in²). Number lines to correspond with numbers on graph pattern.

3. Decide on a starting point, for instance the neckline. Using the numbers as a guide, locate its position in the rectangle both horizontally and vertically, and mark the position with an X or a dot. Continue to mark all the points which cross the lines, and also the points

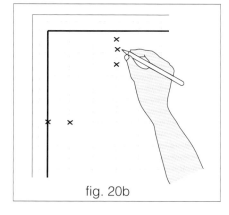

fig. 20b

where the lines change direction, with an X or a dot (Fig. 20b).

4. Join the marks you have made using a ruler or a tape measure. Transfer all the pattern markings and cut out the pattern (Fig. 20c).

fig. 20c

TAKING MEASUREMENTS (Fig. 21)

1. *Chest:* Take the measurement across the widest part of the back, under the arms and across the chest. Keep the tape measure flat and straight. Exhale before measuring.

2. *Waist:* Tie a piece of string around your waist, allowing it to roll to your natural waistline. Exhale completely before measuring.

3. *Hips:* Take the measurement around the fullest part of the buttocks, noting the distance from the waist. Keeping your fingers on the tape measure, position it so that you are able to climb in and out of the tape measure comfortably.

4. *Shoulder length:* Measure the distance from the hollow of the collarbone to the end of the shoulder.

5. *Arm length:* Keeping the elbow bent, measure the distance from the top of the arm (where the shoulder ends), along the outside of the arm, down to the wrist.

6. *Back length:* Measure the distance from the bump at the back of the neck to the required length of the finished garment.

7. *Inner leg:* Measure the distance from the crotch to the ankle.

8. *Crotch:* Measure from the centre front waist, between the legs and through to the centre back waist.

ESTIMATING THE AMOUNT OF FABRIC REQUIRED

After taking all the measurements, drawing the patterns onto graph paper, and drawing in the style of the sleeve and the colour blocking, you must determine how much fabric of each colour is needed. Place the cut-out pattern pieces on a table or a sheet of white paper the same width as the fabric, and measure the length of the pattern pieces. Take into account that some pattern pieces must be placed on a fold or on the bias. Also remember to add the seam allowance.

If you are using stretch fabric, add approximately 5–10 cm (2–4 in) when measuring, in case the fabric shrinks when washed.

FABRICS

There are two types of stretch fabric:

Single knits consist of one layer of fabric, and the RS and WS of the fabric can easily be distinguished. They are most suitable for draped garments, such as T-shirts, shorts and also for tracksuits that have details such as pleats or gathers.

Double knits consist of two layers of fabric and are therefore very sturdy. The RS and WS cannot easily be distinguished. These knits will not fluff or create baggy knees. They are also hard-wearing, and they give a most professional appearance.

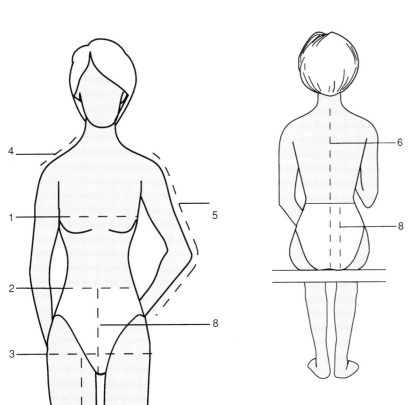

fig. 21

SYMBOLS ON PATTERNS

- Straight grain

- Place on fold

- Hem line

- Pattern size:

Small

Medium

Large

Extra large

RIB TRIM

Rib trim must never be pre-washed, as this will affect the elasticity and you will therefore not be able to measure it accurately.

There are several different types of rib trim, varying in fibre composition and stretch. Although rib trim can usually be classified, it is mostly composed of different fibres. Sometimes Lycra is woven into the rib trim to help it retain its shape. You can see the Lycra if you stretch the rib trim – it is the white elastic threads woven into the rib trim.

As cotton rib trim tends to lose its elasticity when it is washed, it is more suitable for use on garments such as T-shirts. However, nylon rib trim retains its shape when washed and is suitable for tracksuits.

Acrylic rib trim retains its shape when it has been washed and it can be used equally successfully for T-shirts as well as tracksuits.

WADDING

Approximately 3 mm (⅛ in) thick and made from 100% polyester, wadding is generally used for making both garments and soft furnishings. It is washed according to standard washing procedures and it does not need any special treatment. Wadding can be washed either in the washing machine or by hand, and should preferably not be tumble dried. Do not iron it either.

FASTENERS

ELASTIC

Elastic is used to finish off waists and sleeves, and is generally either woven or knitted.

• Knitted elastic consists of a rubber core covered in a nylon yarn, and it has more elasticity than the woven variety of elastic.

• Woven elastic is more tightly woven than knitted elastic, and a greater amount of yarn is used to manufacture woven elastic. Lycra is covered with nylon yarn, and although it does not stretch as much as knitted elastic does, it is definitely stronger and it lasts longer.

ZIPPERS

Open-end and reversible open-end zippers are generally used when making tracksuits.

Zippers are available in polyester, metal and nylon. Polyester zippers are most suitable for skirts and soft furnishings, while metal and nylon zippers are used for jackets, coats and leisurewear. Nylon zippers are very strong and durable. Lightweight zippers are most often used for polyester cotton, while medium-weight and heavyweight zippers are suitable for coats and jackets made from denim or cotton.

CORD

Cotton or nylon cord is available in various thicknesses. Cotton cord is usually cheaper than nylon cord, but it shrinks when it is washed. Nylon cord is strong and durable and is therefore suitable for making piping and to use as a fastener.

POPPERS

These are decorative snap fasteners which are available in various sizes and colours. While ordinary snaps are sewn on, poppers are pushed through the fabric and therefore involve no sewing. Depending on the purpose for which they are needed, either lightweight or heavy-weight poppers can be used.

EQUIPMENT USED FOR PROJECTS

GRAPH PAPER

This is a special paper which has two square sizes ruled on the same sheet. The smaller squares are 1 cm² (⅜ in²) and the larger (usually darker) squares are 5 cm² (2 in²). This paper varies in size and is used to design patterns and also to draw patterns to full size.

DRESSMAKERS' TRACING PAPER

There are several types of strong tracing paper available which can be used for transferring patterns, for example Vi-Trace or Poli-Trace. This type of paper is sold by the metre (yard) at both haberdashers and needlework shops, and does not tear or crease easily.

QUILTERS' RULER

This ruler measures 60 cm (24 in) in length and 10 cm or 12 cm (4 in or 4¾ in) in width, with these markings shown lengthwise and widthwise. The ruler also indicates various angles, such as 45° and 90°. The quilters' ruler is most useful for all needlework purposes.

ROTARY CUTTER

The rotary cutter is equipped with a rotating blade with which the fabric is cut, thus eliminating the use of pins and weights to hold the pattern in place. They are available in two sizes, the larger of which is more suitable for needlework. The same cutter can be used by a right- and a left-handed person. Always cut on a cutting board to protect the surface of your table and extend the life span of your blade. Hold the rotary cutter upright when cutting.

CUTTING BOARD

The cutting board is made from polypropylene and protects the surface underneath. They are available in sizes of 1 m x 1 m (about 1 yd x 1 yd) or 1 m x 2 m (about 1 yd x 2 yd). The cutting board can be permanently glued to your working surface, or it can be opened out on a carpet and rolled up after use.

SCISSORS

Always use a good quality pair of sewing scissors, with sharp blades for precision cutting. The size of the pair of scissors you choose will depend on the type of project which you are undertaking.

PINS

Stainless steel pins will not rust. Preferably use 2.5 cm (1 in) long pins, with coloured heads which can be seen more clearly on the fabric. Discard any rusted and bent pins immediately.

TAPE MEASURE

It is preferable to use a non-stretch fibreglass tape measure. A tape measure is usually 150 cm (about 1½ yd) long, marked on both sides, with two metal ends.

To measure awkward angles and curves, it is very useful to position the tape measure on its side (upright), so that it can be bent around the curve to be measured.

HANDY GAUGE

This metal or plastic ruler is 15 cm (6 in) long. It is equipped with a sliding marker to facilitate taking small measurements such as hems, seams or buttonholes.

STITCH SEALANT

This is a transparent liquid (such as Fray Check) which is used to seal thread ends in order to prevent them from fraying. Apply one drop only and set aside for a few seconds to dry completely. It does not melt when ironed, neither does it scratch or irritate the skin. Stitch sealant is used at the end of an overlocking stitch to prevent the stitching from fraying or unravelling. It may also be used to control runs in stockings, to reinforce buttonholes and prevent them from fraying, or to secure the threads with which buttons have been sewn on to prevent the buttons from coming undone. Always test the stitch sealant on a small piece of scrap fabric first, as it may slightly discolour the fabric and leave a permanent mark.

MARKING TOOLS

Special marking pens are used to transfer markings from the pattern onto your fabric. They are usually water soluble and can be obtained from most haberdashers. The purple pen markings will disappear within approximately 48 hours, depending on the type of fabric you use. The blue markings, however, have to be washed out in cold water. Do not use the blue pen on delicate fabrics, as washing will leave water marks. All markings must be removed before pressing the garment.

Marking pencils and tailors' chalk are also available in a variety of shapes, sizes and colours. They have sharp points and can be used directly on the fabric. The marks can easily be rubbed off afterwards.

NOTE: Leftover bits of soap make an excellent substitute for tailors' chalk when marking fabric. Soap washes out easily.

BIAS BINDING MAKER

This gadget is used for making your own bias binding which is then sewn onto the garment with the sewing machine. To make your own binding, feed the pre-cut bias strip of fabric through the gadget starting at the widest end. The folded bias binding will then emerge on the other side. Iron the binding as you pull it out, holding the gadget by its handle. For the 25 mm (1 in) bias binding maker, cut strips of fabric approximately 48 mm (2 in) wide, and for the 12 mm (½ in) bias binding maker, cut strips of fabric about 25 mm (1 in) wide.

BINDING FOOT

Use bias binding which you have made with a bias binding maker as described above. Feed the folded bias binding through the binding foot, and adjust according to the width of the binding. Sew to the fabric, using your sewing machine and straight stitch, stitch length 2–3.

SOME OF THE PRODUCTS YOU WILL NEED TO MAKE THE GARMENTS

TRACKSUITS

By using just a small amount of initiative, originality and creativity, tracksuits can easily be made and trimmed to be quite original and very interesting.

The same basic pattern is used for making all the tracksuits in this book. You choose your own style, drawing in the desired style lines in order to design your own pattern. Then you decide on the type of trimming you would like to use on your tracksuit, which will depend on the purpose for which it is to be made, for instance casual or sportswear.

First, I shall describe some of the different ways in which the neck, sleeve and waist edges can be finished, and afterwards I shall explain how the different styles are made up, using various trimmings. Give free rein to your imagination – and enjoy it!

TRACKSUIT TOPS

NECK FINISHES
ROUND NECK WITH RIB TRIM

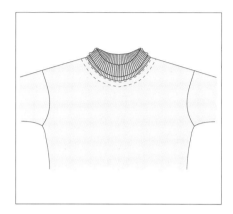

1. Stitch shoulder seams together, so that the neck forms a circle.

2. To determine the length of the rib trim for the neck, place the shoulder seams together and lay the top flat. Measure the neck accurately by positioning the tape measure on its side (Fig. 1). Multiply this measurement by two to determine the total measurement of the neck. Cut the rib trim to two-thirds of the total neck measurement.

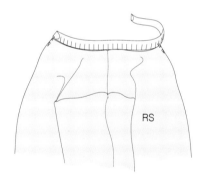

fig. 1

3. To determine width of rib trim for neck, measure twice desired width (e.g. 2.5 cm [1 in] x 2 = 5 cm [2 in]), adding 1 cm (⅜ in) seam allowance on either side of the rib trim (5 cm + 2 cm = 7 cm [2 in + ¾ in = 2¾ in]).

4. With the right sides together, stitch the short ends of the rib trim neatly together using three- or four-thread overlocking.

NOTE: If neck measures less than 30 cm (12 in), for instance on a child's tracksuit, cut rib trim 30 cm (12 in) long, otherwise neck opening will not be wide enough to fit over child's head.

5. Fold the rib trim in half and **quarter pin mark. Quarter pin mark** the round neck (p. 12).

6. Turn the RS of the top to the inside. With raw edges together, place the rib trim inside the top on the RS of the neck edge. Position seam of rib trim on the centre back of neck and pin. Continue pinning, matching up pin marks (Fig. 2).

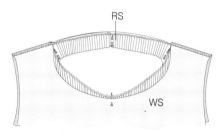

fig. 2

7. Stitch with four-thread overlocking, keeping rib trim on top (Fig. 3). Secure thread ends with stitch sealant.

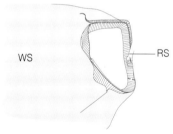

fig. 3

• OPTIONAL: Top stitch RS of top, 3 mm (⅛ in) from seam, using sewing machine and a 4 mm (¼ in) twin needle, stitch length 4–5 (Fig. 4).

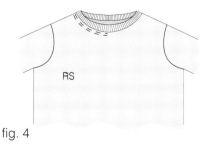

fig. 4

ROUND NECK WITH SELF TRIM

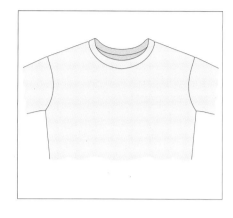

1. Stitch shoulder seams together, so that the neck forms a circle.

2. To determine the length of the neck band, place the shoulder seams together and lay the top flat. Measure the neck, positioning the tape measure on its side (Fig. 1). Multiply this measurement by two to determine the total neck measurement. Cut neck band to total neck measurement minus 7 cm (2¾ in).

3. To determine width of neck band, measure twice desired width (e.g. 2.5 cm [1 in] x 2 = 5 cm [2 in]), adding 1 cm (⅜ in) seam allowance on either side of neck band (5 cm + 2 cm = 7 cm [2 in + ¾ in = 2¾ in]).

4. With the right sides together, stitch the short ends of the neck band together using three- or four-thread overlocking.

5. Fold the neck band in half and **quarter pin mark. Quarter pin mark** the round neck (p. 12).

6. Turn RS of the top to the inside. With raw edges together, place the neck band inside the top on the RS of the neck edge. Position seam of neck band on the centre back of neck and pin. Continue pinning, matching up pin marks (Fig. 2).

7. Stitch together, using four-thread overlocking and keeping the neck band on top (Fig. 3). Secure the thread ends with stitch sealant.

• OPTIONAL: Top stitch on the right sides of the top, 3 mm (⅛ in) away from the seam, using the sewing machine and a 4 mm (¼ in) twin needle, stitch length approximately 4–5 (Fig. 4, p. 26).

OVERLAPPING V-NECK WITH RIB OR SELF TRIM

1. Press a fold on the centre front of the top front. Mark the desired depth of the V on the centre front and draw a straight line from this mark to the shoulder line. Cut out the V (Fig. 1). Mark the centre back with a pin.

TOPS WITH ROUND NECKS, P. 26

fig. 1

NOTE: If finished width of rib trim or fabric strip is wider than 3 cm (1¼ in), the extra width must be cut away at neck edge of shoulder seam. If neck band is 5 cm (2 in) wide, for instance, you will need to cut away 2 cm (¾ in) at neck edge on shoulder seam (Fig. 2).

2. Stay stitch the V on the RS of the top front if you are using stretch fabric, to reinforce it and prevent it from losing its shape. Stitch 6 mm (¼ in) from the raw edge, using the

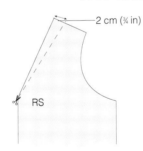

fig. 2

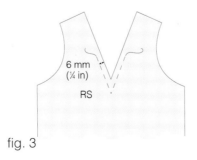

fig. 3

sewing machine and straight stitch, stitch length 2–3 (Fig. 3). Insert a pin about 5 cm (2 in) from the shoulder seam on either side of the top front for adults, and about 3 cm (1¼ in) for children (Fig. 4).

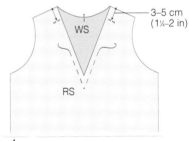

fig. 4

3. To determine length of rib trim or fabric strip for neck, place shoulder seams together and lay top flat. Measure neck and multiply this measurement by two to determine total neck measurement. Cut rib trim or fabric strip to length of total neck measurement plus 10 cm (4 in).

4. To determine width of neck band, cut rib trim or fabric strip to twice desired width (e.g. 3 cm [1¼ in] x 2 = 6 cm [2½ in]), adding a 1 cm (⅜ in) seam allowance on either side of the neck band (6 cm + 2 cm = 8 cm [2½ in + ¾ in = 3¼ in]).

5. Fold neck band in half lengthways, WS together. Fold in half widthways and mark fold with a pin.

6. Place rib trim or fabric strip on RS of neck, matching pin with centre back of neck. Pin into position.

7. Stretch neck band 2–3 cm (¾–1¼ in) on either side between centre back and the pin on front, and pin into position so that rib trim or fabric strip lies flat against back of neck.

8. Continue pinning rib trim or fabric strip to one side of neck up to centre front, without stretching neck band. Continue pinning neck band to the other side of neck up to 5 cm (2 in) from the centre front (Fig. 5).

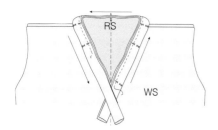

fig. 5

9. Stitch neck band to neck using sewing machine and straight stitch, stitch length 2–3, starting at centre front, around the neck, and ending 5 cm (2 in) from the centre front on the other side (Fig. 5). Clip to the stitching on the centre front (Fig. 6).

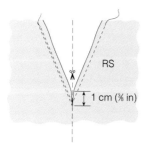

fig. 6

10. Turn the top inside out and pull both ends of the neck band through to the WS, so that they form a V on the WS (Fig. 7). Pin into position. Cut away excess neck band (Fig. 7).

11. Working on WS, stitch remaining 5 cm (2 in) of neck band into position

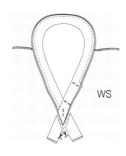

fig. 7

using sewing machine and straight stitch, stitch length 2–3. The neck band forms a V on the RS (Fig. 8).

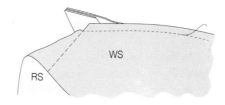

fig. 8

12. Finish raw edge using three- or four-thread overlocking (Fig. 9). Secure thread ends with stitch sealant.

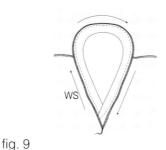

fig. 9

MITRED V-NECK WITH RIB OR SELF TRIM

1. Press a fold on the centre front of the top front. Mark the desired

depth of the V on the centre front and draw a straight line from this mark to the shoulder line. Cut out the V (Fig. 1, p. 27). Mark the centre back with a pin.

NOTE: If the width of the rib trim or the fabric strip is wider than 3 cm (1¼ in), the extra width must be cut away at the neck edge of the shoulder seam. If the neck band is 5 cm (2 in) wide, you will need to cut away 2 cm (¾ in) (Fig. 2, p. 27).

2. Stay stitch V on RS of top front if using stretch fabric, to reinforce it and prevent it from losing its shape. Stitch 6 mm (¼ in) from raw edge, using sewing machine and straight stitch, stitch length 2–3 (Fig. 3, p. 27).

3. Insert pin 5 cm (2 in) from shoulder on each side for adults; 3 cm (1¼ in) for children (Fig. 4, p. 27).

4. To determine length of rib trim or fabric strip for neck, place shoulder seams together and lay top flat. Measure neck and multiply this measurement by two to determine total neck measurement. Cut rib trim or fabric strip to length of total neck measurement plus 10 cm (4 in).

5. To determine width of neck band, cut rib trim or fabric strip to twice desired width (e.g. 3 cm [1¼ in] x 2 = 6 cm [2½ in]), adding a 1 cm (⅜ in) seam allowance on either side of neck band (6 cm + 2 cm = 8 cm [2½ in + ¾ in = 3¼ in]).

6. Fold neck band in half lengthways, WS together. Fold in half widthways and mark fold with a pin. Place rib trim or fabric strip on RS of neck, matching up pin with centre back of neck. Pin into position. Stretch neck band 2–3 cm (¾–1¼ in) between the centre back and the pin on the front, and pin into position on both sides so that it lies flat against back of neck.

7. Continue pinning the rib trim or fabric strip to both sides of the neck

up to the centre front, without stretching the neck band (Fig. 10).

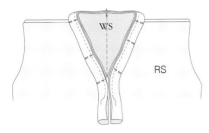

fig. 10

8. Stitch neck band to neck using sewing machine and straight stitch, stitch length 2–3, starting at centre front, around neck, and back to centre front (Fig. 10). Clip to stitching on centre front (Fig. 6, p. 28). Turn top inside out. Lay top flat, with neck band at the top (Fig. 11).

fig. 11

9. Using a ruler and marking pen or tailors' chalk, draw a line on the centre front of the neck band to form an extension of the centre front line of the top (Fig. 11).

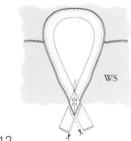

fig. 12

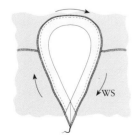

fig. 13

TRACKSUIT TOPS WITH V-NECKS, P. 27–29

10. Stitch the neck band together along the marked line, using sewing machine and straight stitch, stitch length about 2–3. Open out and press the V on the wrong side. Cut away excess ends (Fig. 12).

11. Finish the edges of the neck using three- or four-thread overlocking (Fig. 13). Secure the thread ends with stitch sealant.

TAB FRONT WITH COLLAR

1. Cut out of the fabric: back, front, 2 x sleeve and 1 x collar (on the fold) and 2 x facing.
Cut out of the interfacing: 2 facings and collar (Fig. 1).
Cut out of the tracing paper: stay (Fig. 2, p. 30).

fig. 1a

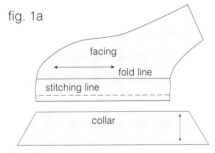

fig. 1b

• OPTIONAL: To create a rugby jersey look, use non-stretch fabric in a contrasting colour to make the collar and the facings.

2. Iron the interfacing onto the two facings and the collar (Fig. 1). Using

a marking pen or tailors' chalk, draw in lines on stay and facings, working accurately (Fig. 2).

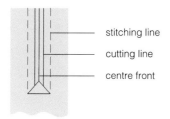

fig. 2

3. Press a fold on centre front of top. Mark fold on the WS using a marking pen or tailors' chalk. Position stay on WS of the top, matching up the centre front lines (Fig. 3).

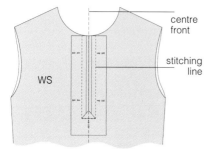

fig. 3

4. Stitch along stitching line of stay using sewing machine and straight stitch, stitch length 2–3 (Fig. 3).

5. Cut along cutting lines through both the top and the stay (Fig. 4).

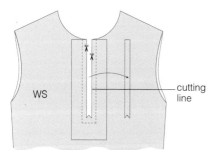

fig. 4

6. Finish the outer edges and the shoulder edges of the facings using three-thread overlocking.

7. Pin the facings to the front, RS and raw edges together, and stitch the facings into position, once again along the stitching line (Fig. 5).

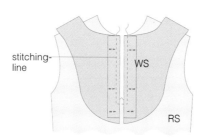

fig. 5

8. Tear out the stay. Clip to the corners at the bottom end of the facings (Fig. 6).

fig. 6

9. Fold facings over to WS along fold lines and pin into position. Lay top flat, with RS up. Overlap facings and pin into position. For men, the right facing should overlap the left (Fig. 7a). For ladies, the left facing should overlap the right (Fig. 7b).

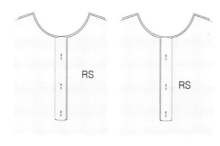

fig. 7b   fig. 7a

10. Fold the front upwards at the bottom end of the tab, RS together,

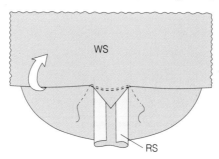

fig. 8

and stitch bottom end of facings down using straight stitch. Stitch over the previous stitching (Fig. 8).

11. Using the sewing machine and straight stitch, stitch length 2–3, stitch a reinforcing square on the right side at the bottom end of the facings (Fig. 9).

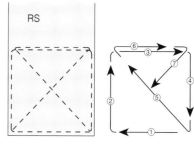

fig. 9

12. Pin the shoulder seams together, RS together, and stitch using four-thread overlocking (Fig. 10). Press the shoulder seams backwards.

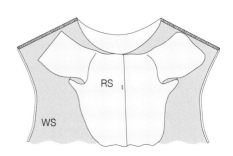

fig. 10

13. Fold collar in half, right sides together, and stitch up ends using sewing machine and straight stitch. Trim corners diagonally, cutting away excess fabric (Fig. 11). Turn collar right side out.

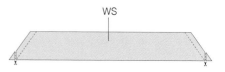

fig. 11

• OPTIONAL: Top stitch collar on right side, 6 mm from the edge. Use the sewing machine and straight stitch, stitch length 3–4.

14. Using the sewing machine and straight stitch, stitch length 3–4, stay stitch the neck edge 6 mm (¼ in) from edge, from one facing seam to the other, to prevent the neck from losing its shape (Fig. 12).

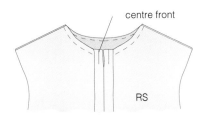

fig. 12

15. Mark centre back of the collar and top with pins. With the interfaced side of the collar towards the top, pin the centre back of the collar to the centre back of the top.

16. Using a marking pen or tailors' chalk, mark centre of both tabs halfway between stitching line and fold line. This is centre front (Fig. 12).

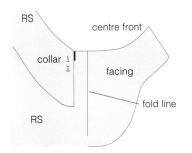

fig. 13

17. Pin the ends of the collar to the centre front marks on tabs (Fig. 13). Fold the facing back over the collar along the fold line and pin it into position (Fig. 14). Repeat this step for the other side.

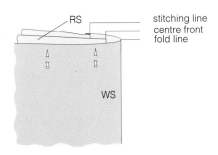

fig. 14

18. Using the sewing machine and straight stitch, stitch collar to neck opening from centre back to fold at end of facing. Repeat for other side. Finish the neck edge using three- or four-thread overlocking (Fig. 15).

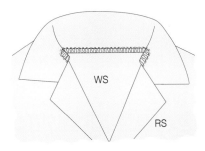

fig. 15

19. Turn the facings to the wrong side and attach three or four poppers. Sew the shoulder seams of the facings to the shoulder seams of the top using an overhand stitch.

NOTE: If the facings are at all visible through the fabric, the facings may be cut away, right-up against the tab, and then stitched down using the sewing machine and straight stitch, stitch length approximately 2–3, right against the edge of the tab on the right side.

TAB FRONT WITH RIB TRIM

1. Cut out of the fabric: back, front and 2 x sleeve (on the fold) and 2 x facing.
Cut out of the interfacing: 2 facings (Fig. 1a, p. 29).
Cut out of the tracing paper: stay (Fig. 2, p. 30).

• OPTIONAL: Use fabric in a contrasting colour for the rib trim and facings. Non-stretch fabric may also be used for the facings.

2. Iron interfacing onto the facings (Fig. 1, p. 29). Using a marking pen or tailors' chalk, draw in the lines on the stay and facings, working very accurately (Fig. 2, p. 30). Press a fold on the centre front of the top. Mark the fold on the WS using a marking pen or tailors' chalk.

3. Position stay on WS of top, matching up the centre front lines. Stitch along stitching line of stay using sewing machine and straight stitch, stitch length 2–3 (Fig. 3, p. 30).

4. Cut along the cutting lines through both the top and the stay (Fig. 4, p. 30). Finish the outer edges and shoulder edges of the facings using three-thread overlocking.

5. Pin the facings to the front, RS and raw edges together, and stitch the facings into position, once again along the stitching line (Fig. 5, p. 30).

6. Clip to corners at bottom end of the facings (Fig. 6, p. 30). Fold the facings over to WS along fold lines and pin into position. Remove stay.

7. Lay top flat, with RS up. Overlap facings and pin into position. For men, the right facing should overlap the left. For ladies, the left should overlap the right (Fig. 7, p. 30).

8. Fold front upwards at bottom end of the tab, RS together, and stitch the bottom end of the facings down using straight stitch. Stitch over the previous stitching (Fig. 8, p. 30).

9. Using the sewing machine and straight stitch, stitch length 2–3, stitch a reinforcing square on RS at bottom end of facings (Fig. 9, p. 30).

10. Pin the shoulder seams together, RS together, and stitch using four-thread overlocking (Fig. 10, p. 30). Press shoulder seams backwards.

11. To determine length of rib trim, place shoulder seams together and lay the top flat. Measure the neck, positioning tape measure on its side. Cut rib trim to two-thirds the length of the total neck measurement.

12. To determine width of rib trim, measure twice desired width (e.g. 2.5 cm [1 in] x 2 = 5 cm [2 in]), adding 1 cm (⅜ in) seam allowance on either side of rib trim (5 cm + 2 cm = 7 cm [2 in + ¾ in = 2¾ in]).

13. Fold rib trim in half and mark centre with a pin. Also mark centre back of the top with a pin. Pin the centre of the rib trim to the centre back of the top. Using a marking pen or tailors' chalk, mark centre of both tabs halfway between the stitching line and the fold line. This is the centre front (Fig. 16).

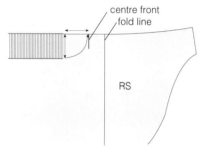

fig. 16

14. Pin ends of rib trim into position 2.5 cm (1 in) from centre front (i.e. the width of the rib trim) on the tabs (Fig. 16). Pull folded ends of rib trim to the centre front on the tabs and pin into position (Fig. 17).

15. Stitch ends of rib trim into position using sewing machine and zig-zag stitch, stitch length 2 and width 1. Cut away excess rib trim (Fig. 17).

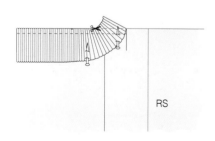

fig. 17

16. Fold the facing back over the rib trim along the fold line and pin it into position (Fig. 14, p. 31). Repeat for the other side.

17. Using the sewing machine and straight stitch, stitch length 2–3, stitch the rib trim to neck opening from the centre back to the fold at the end of the facing. Repeat for the other side.

18. Finish the neck edge using three- or four-thread overlocking (Fig. 15, p. 31). Turn the facings to the wrong side and attach three or four poppers. Stitch the facings to the shoulder seams.

EASY TAB FRONT WITH COLLAR OR RIB TRIM

1. Use the pattern piece for the front. Draw a horizontal line on the front for blocking, and cut through, making sure that the horizontal line does not coincide with the bust.

2. Place the top piece on tracing paper and pin into position.

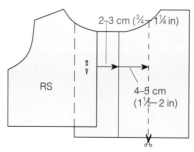

fig. 1

3. Add 2–3 cm (¾–1¼ in) to centre front, drawing a line parallel to the centre front. This forms the tab. Draw a second line, parallel to the fold line and 4–5 cm (1½–2 in) away, to form the facing (Fig. 1).

4. Fold tracing paper in half along fold line and cut along neckline to shape neckline of facing (Fig. 1).

5. Fold the fabric in half and pin the pattern piece onto the fabric. Mark a 1 cm (⅜ in) seam allowance on the fabric using tailors' chalk, and cut out. Mark WS of fabric with tailors' chalk if not easily distinguishable.

6. Cut collar out of tracing paper and pin into position. Mark 1 cm (⅜ in) seam allowance on the fabric using tailors' chalk. Cut out collar. Remember that rib trim can also be used.

7. Finish facing edges with three- or four-thread overlocking.

8. Pin the shoulder seams together, RS together, and stitch using four-thread overlocking (Fig. 10, p. 30). Press the shoulder seams backwards.

IF YOU ARE USING A COLLAR
9. Fold collar in half, RS together, and stitch up the ends. Trim corners diagonally, cutting away excess fabric (Fig. 11, p. 30). Turn collar RS out.

10. Using the sewing machine and straight stitch, stitch length 3–4, stay stitch the neck edge 6 mm (¼ in) from edge, from one facing seam to the other, to prevent the neck from losing its shape (Fig. 12, p. 31).

11. Mark centre back of collar and top with pins. With interfaced side of collar towards top, pin centre back of collar to centre back of top.

12. Using a marking pen or tailors' chalk, mark centre of both tabs halfway between stitching line and fold line. This is centre front (Fig. 12, p. 31). Pin ends of collar to centre front marks on tabs (Fig. 13, p. 31). Fold facing back over collar along the fold line and pin (Fig. 14, p. 31). Repeat for other side.

RUGBY-STYLE TOPS WITH TAB FRONT, P. 29–34

13. Using the sewing machine and straight stitch, stitch collar to neck opening from centre back to fold at end of facing. Repeat for other side.

IF YOU ARE USING RIB TRIM

9. To determine length of rib trim, place shoulder seams together and lay the top flat. Measure the neck, positioning tape measure on its side. Cut rib trim to two-thirds the length of the total neck measurement.

10. To determine width of rib trim, measure twice the desired width (e.g. 2.5 cm [1 in] x 2 = 5 cm [2 in]), adding 1 cm (⅜ in) seam allowance on either side of the rib trim (5 cm + 2 cm = 7 cm [2 in + ¾ in = 2¾ in]).

11. Fold rib trim in half and mark centre with a pin. Also mark centre back of the top with a pin. Pin the centre of the rib trim to the centre back of the top. Using a marking pen or tailors' chalk, mark centre of both tabs halfway between the stitching line and the fold line. This is the centre front (Fig. 12, p. 31).

12. Pin the ends of the rib trim into position 2.5 cm (1 in) from centre front (i.e. the width of the rib trim) on the tabs (Fig. 16, p. 32). Pull the folded ends of the rib trim to the centre front on the tabs and pin them into position (Fig. 17, p. 32). Stitch ends of rib trim into position using sewing machine and zig-zag stitch, stitch length 2 and width 1. Cut away excess rib trim (Fig. 17, p. 32). Fold facing back over the rib trim along the fold line and pin into position (Fig. 14, p. 31). Repeat for the other side.

13. Using the sewing machine and straight stitch, stitch rib trim to neck opening from centre back to end of the facing. Repeat for the other side.

COLLAR OR RIB TRIM

14. Finish the neck edge using three- or four-thread overlocking (Fig. 15, p. 31). Turn the facings to the wrong side and attach three or four poppers.

15. Stitch the shoulder seams of the facings to the shoulder seams of the tracksuit top, using a neat overhand stitch.

NOTE: If the facings are at all visible through the fabric, the facings may carefully be cut away to right up against the tab and then they may be stitched down right against the edge of the tab on the right side, using the sewing machine and straight stitch, stitch length approximately 2–3.

NECK OPENING WITH CORD

1. To determine the length of the fabric strip, place the shoulder seams together and lay the top flat. Measure the neck, positioning the tape measure on its side. Multiply this measurement by two to determine the total neck measurement. Cut the fabric strip to the length of the neck measurement plus 2 cm (¾ in) for seam allowances.

2. The width of the fabric strip for the neck is 14–18 cm (5½–7 in).

3. Stitch the short ends of the fabric strip for the neck together, with the right sides together, using three- or four thread overlocking.

4. Fold the fabric strip in half lengthways, with the right sides together, and then in half widthways. Mark the fold line and the centre front on the right side using a marking pen or tailors' chalk.

5. Using the sewing machine and buttonhole foot, make a horizontal buttonhole on a single layer of fabric, 1 cm (⅜ in) from fold line on centre front, 2 cm (¾ in) in length.

6. To make casing for cord, fold fabric in half and mark 2 cm (¾ in) from fold line, using tailors' chalk. Stitch along marked line, using a sewing machine and straight stitch.

7. **Quarter pin mark** the fabric strip. **Quarter pin mark** the round neck (p. 12).

8. Turn RS of top to inside. With raw edges together, place fabric strip inside top on RS of neck edge. Position the seam of the fabric strip on the centre back of neck and pin, matching up pin marks (Fig. 3).

9. Stitch together, using four-thread overlocking and keeping the fabric strip on top (Fig. 4). Secure the thread ends with stitch sealant.

ZIPPER WITH FLATLOCKING

Use either a collar, rib trim, or a hood for finishing the neck of a tracksuit top with a zipper.

1. Cut out the front of the top along the zipper line.

2. Pin WS of the zipper to WS of the fabric. Fold top end of the zipper tape over to the WS of the zipper. Pin into position (Fig. 1).

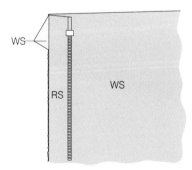

fig. 1

3. Stitch using **flatlocking** (any variation). Secure the thread ends with stitch sealant. Use finishing of your choice to finish neck of tracksuit.

HOODS

Hoods are both fashionable and useful – not only do they look very stylish, but at the same time they keep one warm in winter. Hoods are mainly used on leisurewear, and they provide an effective finish for the garment.

Hoods can be sewn onto the neck edge, or they can be made separately and attached to the neck edge of the top by means of Velcro or poppers. Finish the neck edge with bias binding if you are making the hood separately and attaching it to the tracksuit or jacket with Velcro or poppers. Use either the bias binder on the five-thread overlocker (p. 10) or the binding foot and straight stitch, stitch length 3–4, on the sewing machine (p. 23).

HOOD WITH RIB TRIM

1. Trace the hood onto tracing paper without a hemline. Cut out and pin onto fabric. Using tailors' chalk, mark a 1 cm (⅜ in) seam allowance on the fabric all round the hood (Fig. 1).

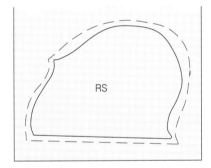

fig. 1

2. Cut two hood sections out of the fabric. Stitch the hood seam using **flatlocking** (any variation) or three- or four-thread overlocking.

3. To determine the length of the rib trim for the face edge, lay the hood flat. Measure the face edge, positioning the tape measure on its side (Fig. 2). Multiply this measurement by two to determine the total measurement. Cut the rib trim to three-quarters the length of the total measurement. The width of the rib trim is 7 cm (2¾ in).

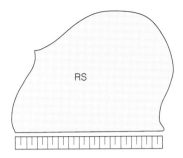

fig. 2

4. Fold the rib trim in half and **quarter pin mark**. **Quarter pin mark** the hood (p. 12).

5. Place the rib trim on the RS of the hood, matching up the pin marks. Pin into position. Stitch, using four-thread overlocking and keeping the rib trim at the top.

6. Pin the hood to the neck of the top, RS together, and stitch using four-thread overlocking.

SINGLE HOOD WITH CORD

1. Trace hood onto tracing paper. Cut out pattern and pin it onto the fabric. Using tailors' chalk, mark a 1 cm (⅜ in) seam allowance on the fabric all round the hood (Fig. 1).

2. Cut out two hood sections. Stitch, using **flatlocking** (any variation) or three- or four-thread overlocking.

3. Mark 3 cm (1¼ in) from bottom edge and 1.5 cm (⅝ in) from face edge on either side for buttonholes. These must be vertical, and 2 cm (¾ in) in length (Fig. 3).

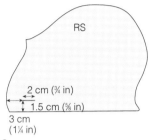

fig. 3

4. Make the buttonholes, using the sewing machine and buttonhole foot. Mark 2.5 cm (1 in) from face edge and make casing for cord, using a **flatlocked hem** (Fig. 19, p. 19).

5. Pin the hood to the neck of the top, RS together, and stitch using four-thread overlocking. Thread the cord through the casing.

A SELECTION OF HOODS

DOUBLE HOOD WITH PIPING AND CORD

1. Trace hood onto tracing paper. Cut out pattern and pin onto fabric. Using tailors' chalk, mark 1 cm (⅜ in) seam allowance on the fabric all round the hood (Fig. 1, p. 35). Cut four hood sections out of the fabric.

2. Using tape guide attachment and piping foot (p. 9), or zipper foot and straight stitch, stitch length 2–3, on the sewing machine, stitch the hood seam, inserting piping (Fig. 4). Repeat for the other hood.

3. Using tape guide attachment and piping foot (p. 9), or the sewing machine and zipper foot, stitch hoods together along the face edge seam, inserting piping (Fig. 4).

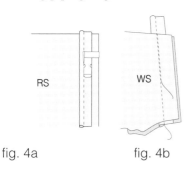

fig. 4a   fig. 4b

4. Mark 3 cm (1¼ in) from bottom edge and 1.5 cm (⅝ in) from face edge on either side of one hood for buttonholes. These must be vertical, and 2 cm (¾ in) in length (Fig. 3, p. 35). Make buttonholes, using sewing machine and buttonhole foot.

5. To make casing for cord, mark 2.5 cm (1 in) from face edge, using tailors' chalk. Stitch along marked line, using a sewing machine and straight stitch, stitch length 2–3.

6. Pin hood to neck, RS together, and stitch using four-thread over-locking. Thread cord through casing.

HOOD WITH ELASTIC

1. Trace hood onto tracing paper. Cut out pattern and pin onto fabric. Using tailors' chalk, mark 1 cm (⅜ in) seam allowance on the fabric all round the hood (Fig. 1, p. 35). Cut two hood sections out of the fabric.

2. Stitch the hood seam using **flat-locking** (any variation) or three- or four-thread overlocking.

3. Stitch the elastic to the face edge of the hood, making an **elasticized band** (p. 12). The width of the elastic is 2 cm (¾ in).

4. Pin the hood to the neck of the tracksuit top or jacket, right sides together, and stitch using four-thread overlocking.

SLEEVE FINISHES

RIB TRIM

1. To determine the length of the rib trim for the sleeve, take a loose wrist measurement, or measure around the hand.

2. The width of the rib trim for the sleeve is 12 cm (4¾ in).

3. With RS together, stitch the short ends of the rib trim together using four-thread overlocking.

4. Fold the rib trim in half and **quarter pin mark**. **Quarter pin mark** the sleeve (p. 12).

5. Turn the right side of the top to the inside. With the raw edges together, place the rib trim inside the top on the right side of the sleeve. Position the seam of the rib trim on the sleeve seam and pin. Continue pinning, matching up the pin marks (Fig. 1).

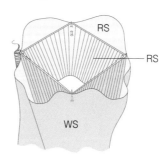

fig. 1

6. Stitch together, using four-thread overlocking and keeping the rib trim on top (Fig. 3, p. 26). Secure the thread ends with stitch sealant.

ELASTIC

1. To determine length of elastic, take the wrist measurement, and cut the elastic to this measurement.

2. Width of the elastic is 2 cm (¾ in).

3. **Join elastic** with three-thread overlocking **to form a circle** (p. 12).

4. Stitch the elastic to the sleeve, making an **elasticized band** (p. 12).

TWIN NEEDLE

Finish sleeve hem, turning under 1–2 cm (⅜–¾ in) of raw edge of the sleeve to WS. Stitch down on RS, using 4 mm (¼ in) twin needle and straight stitch, stitch length 4–5, on sewing machine.

WAIST FINISHES

RIB TRIM

1. To determine the length of the rib trim for the waist:
For adults, hip measurement minus 20 cm (8 in);
For children, hip measurement minus 10 cm (4 in).

2. To determine the width of the rib trim for the waist:
For adults, 18–24 cm (7–9½ in), depending on the length of the top;
For children, 12 cm (4¾ in).

3. Stitch short ends of the rib trim together, with RS together, using four-thread overlocking. Fold the rib trim in half and **quarter pin mark**. **Quarter pin mark** the top (p. 12).

4. Turn RS of top to inside. With raw edges together, place rib trim inside top on RS of waist. Position seam of rib trim on side seam and pin. Continue pinning, matching up pin marks (Fig. 1). Stitch together, using four-thread overlocking and keeping rib trim on top (Fig. 3, p. 26). Secure thread ends with stitch sealant.

WAIST WITH SELF TRIM

1. To determine the length of the fabric strip for the waist, take a firm hip measurement.

2. To determine the width of the fabric strip for the waist:
For adults, 18–24 cm (7–9½ in), depending on the length of the top;
For children, 12 cm (4¾ in).

3. If necessary, join the waist strip to obtain the required length. Stitch the short ends of the strip together, with the right sides together, using four-thread overlocking.

4. Fold the fabric strip in half and **quarter pin mark** (p. 12).

5. **Quarter pin mark** top, with the right side on the inside (p. 12).

6. With the raw edges together, place the fabric strip on the right side of the waist edge. Pin the strip and waist edge together, matching up the pin marks (Fig. 1, p. 36).

7. Stitch together, using four-thread overlocking and keeping the fabric strip on top (Fig. 3, p. 26).

8. Secure the thread ends with stitch sealant to prevent fraying.

ELASTIC
1. To determine the length of the elastic for the waist, take a firm waist measurement, and cut the elastic to this measurement.

2. The width of the elastic for the waist is 2–5 cm (¾–2 in).

3. **Join elastic** with three-thread overlocking **to form a circle** (p. 12).

4. Stitch the elastic to the waist, making an **elasticized band** (p. 12).

CORD
1. Place the side seams of the top together and lay the top flat. Mark the centre front of the top, using a marking pen or tailors' chalk.

2. Make a vertical buttonhole about 2 cm (¾ in) on either side of the centre front of the top, 1.5 cm (⅝ in) from the bottom edge and about 2 cm (¾ in) in length.

3. To make the casing for the cord, fold the raw edge of the fabric back 3 cm (1¼ in) to the WS and stitch, using a sewing machine and straight stitch, stitch length 2–3.

4. Thread cord through the casing.

TWIN NEEDLE
Finish the waist hem, turning under 1–3 cm (⅜–1¼ in) of the raw edge of the waist to the wrong side. Stitch down on the right side, using 4 mm (¼ in) twin needle and straight stitch on the sewing machine.

POCKETS

KANGAROO POCKET
1. To design a kangaroo pocket for a tracksuit, use the complete front of the tracksuit pattern.

2. Mark point A halfway between the underarm point and the bottom edge of the front panel. Draw a line across the front (Fig. 1).

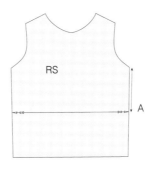

fig. 1

3. Divide line into quarters. These marks indicate top edge of pocket.

4. For the pocket opening, mark point B two-thirds down between the underarm point and the bottom edge on either side (Fig. 2).

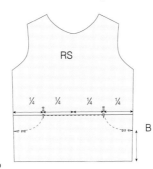

fig. 2

5. Draw a line from the top of the pocket to point B.
• Finish top edge and pocket edges using three-thread overlocking (any variation), piping, or bias binding.
• The pocket edges may also be finished with rib trim. Cut the rib trim to the length of the pocket edge minus 2–3 cm (¾–1¼ in).
• The top edge of the pocket can either be sewn into a horizontal seam (for blocking) or stitched into position on top of the front.
• The pocket can be attached as a whole, or as two separate pockets if a zipper is used.

PATCH POCKET
1. Use pattern 17 on page 79.

2. The pocket can be finished with either three-thread overlocking (any variation) or piping.

3. For three-thread overlocking:
• Finish the rounded and straight edges of the pocket using three-thread overlocking.
• Pin pocket to side seam of front.
• Measure carefully and mark the hand opening (on the side seam edge) (Fig. 3).

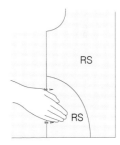

fig. 3

• Stitch the pocket into position along the edges, as shown in Fig. 4, using the sewing machine and straight stitch, stitch length 2–3.

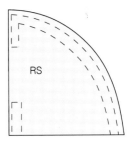

fig. 4

4. For piping:

• Cut out two pocket sections to make one pocket.

• Stitch piping around rounded and straight edges of pocket, using zipper foot and straight stitch, stitch length 2–3, on sewing machine (Fig. 5). To attach piping at outside corner, see page 11. Pin second pocket section to first, RS together, and stitch along the previous stitching.

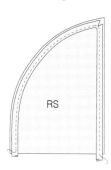

fig. 5

• Trim excess fabric from corners and turn pocket inside out. Pin pocket to side seam of front.

• Measure and mark hand opening on side seam edge (Fig. 3, p. 37).

• Stitch the pocket into position along the edges, as shown in Fig. 4, p. 37, using the sewing machine and straight stitch, stitch length 2–3.

ROUND POCKET

Use pattern 33 on page 94. The pocket is finished with three-thread overlocking (any variation).

• Finish the rounded and straight edges of the pocket using three-thread overlocking.

• Pin pocket onto front. The straight edge forms the hand opening.

• Stitch pocket into position along rounded edge, as shown in Fig. 6, using sewing machine and straight stitch, stitch length 2–3.

fig. 6

TRACKSUIT PANTS

REQUIREMENTS
Stretch fabric
Matching floss and/or polyester cotton thread
Floss or decorative thread
2.5 mm (⅛ in) twin needle for stretch fabric (see page 6)
Marking tools (see page 23)

SEAM ALLOWANCE

1 cm (⅜ in)

STITCHES

Four-thread overlocking (or three-thread overlocking if your machine does not have a four-thread facility)

Straight stitch, stitch length 3–4

PATTERNS

Adults: use patterns 7 and 8 or 9 and 10 on pages 70–73

Children: use patterns 11 and 12 on pages 74 and 75

METHOD

1. Trace pattern pieces onto tracing paper. Mark straight grain on front and back. Pin pattern pieces onto the fabric. Mark 1 cm (⅜ in) seam allowance on fabric and cut out. Mark WS of fabric with tailors' chalk if not easily distinguishable from RS.

2. Pin front and back together, RS together, and stitch inner and outer leg seams from the waist edge to the ankle, using four-thread overlocking. Repeat for the other leg.

• OPTIONAL: The outer leg seam may also be finished with **flatlocking** (any variation) or piping, using tape guide attachment and piping foot or sewing machine and zipper foot. For flatlocking, place WS together.

• OPTIONAL: Fold leg in half and top stitch along centre front, using twin needle and straight stitch, stitch length 3–4, on the sewing machine.

3. Turn one leg to the RS and insert into the other leg, RS together. Stitch crotch seam using four-thread overlocking. Use the finishing of your choice for the waist and ankles.

WAIST FINISHES

ELASTICIZED BAND

Take waist measurement to determine length of elastic. The width is 2–5 cm (¾–2 in). Attach elastic with **elasticized band** (p. 12).

ELASTIC USING THE SEWING MACHINE AND ZIPPER FOOT

1. Finish waist edge with four-thread overlocking. Take waist measurement to determine length of elastic. The width is 2–5 cm (¾–2 in).

2. **Join elastic to form a circle** using three-thread overlocking (p. 12). Place elastic on WS of waist. Fold raw edge of fabric over to WS, width of elastic plus 1 cm (⅜ in).

3. Stitch down next to elastic, using zipper foot and straight stitch, stitch length 3–4, on the sewing machine. Gently pull elastic at the back, so that it lies flat in front of foot, while being gathered at the back (Fig. 1).

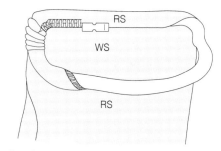

fig. 1

CORD

1. Finish waist edge with four-thread overlocking. Make vertical buttonholes at waist, 2 cm (¾ in) on either side of centre front, using sewing machine and buttonhole foot. These must be 2 cm (¾ in) long.

2. Fold raw edge 3 cm (1¼ in) over to WS. Stitch edge with sewing machine and straight stitch, stitch length 3–4. Thread cord through casing.

ANKLE FINISHES

RIB TRIM

1. To determine length of rib trim for the ankle, take a loose ankle measurement. The width of the rib trim for the ankle is 12 cm (4¾ in).

2. Stitch the short ends of the rib trim together, with the right sides together, using three-thread overlocking. Fold the rib trim in half and **quarter pin mark**. **Quarter pin mark** the ankle (p. 12).

3. Turn RS of pants to the inside. With raw edges together, place the rib trim inside the leg on the RS of the ankle edge. Position seam of the rib trim on the inner leg seam and pin. Continue pinning, matching up the pin marks (Fig. 1, p. 36).

4. Stitch together, using four-thread overlocking and keeping the rib trim on top (Fig. 3, p. 26). Secure the thread ends with stitch sealant.

ELASTIC

1. To determine the length of the elastic: Measure the ankle and cut the elastic to this measurement. The width of the elastic is 2 cm (¾ in).

2. Stitch the elastic to the ankle, making an **elasticized band** (p. 12).

TWIN NEEDLE

Finish the ankle hem, turning under about 1–2 cm (⅜–¾ in) of the raw edge of the ankle to the WS. Stitch down on RS, using the 4 mm (¼ in) twin needle and straight stitch, stitch length 4–5, on the sewing machine.

POCKETS

IN-SEAM POCKET

Use pattern 34 on page 94. Cut out two pieces for each pocket. Pin pockets to front and back of outer leg, RS together. Stitch outer leg seam, RS together, starting at waist, around pocket down to the ankle.

EXTENDED POCKET

This type of pocket is ideal for men's pants, and especially for boys' pants, as it also provides reinforcement at the knees.

1. Extend back of pants along outer leg to the size you want the pocket. Finish edge of the extension using four-thread overlocking.

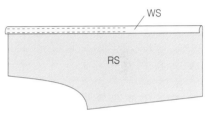

fig. 1

2. Stitch edge of front outer leg seam with four-thread overlocking. Fold in seam allowance on front outer leg seam and stitch two lines of top stitching on the right side using sewing machine and straight stitch, stitch length 3–4 (Fig. 1).

3. Place folded edge on outer leg seam of back. Pin into position. Measure hand opening on outer leg seam, and mark with tailors' chalk.

4. Stitch the pocket of the back to the front outer leg seam using the sewing machine and straight stitch, stitch length 3–4. Stitch two lines of top stitching (Fig. 2).

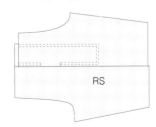

fig. 2

TRACKSUIT BOTTOMS (PANTS) WITH DIFFERENT ANKLE FINISHES

BASIC TRACKSUIT PATTERN

• Use the chest measurement to determine which pattern size to use for the tracksuit top (Fig. 21, p. 21):

Children:
SMALL   2–4 years: Chest 54–58 cm (21–23 in)
MEDIUM 5–8 years: Chest 60–66 cm (24–26 in)
LARGE   9–12 years: Chest 68–74 cm (27–30 in)

Adults:
SMALL   Chest 80 cm (32 in)
MEDIUM Chest 88–92 cm (34–36 in)
LARGE   Chest 97–102 cm (38–40 in)
EXTRA LARGE Chest 107–112 cm (42–44 in)

• Enlarge pattern pieces (front and back) to full scale onto graph paper (p. 20). This is the master pattern which is used to design all variations.

> **NOTE:** No seam allowance has been added to the master pattern. You have to add a 1 cm (⅜ in) seam allowance yourself.

• Mark the straight grain as well as the underarm and shoulder points on each pattern piece (Fig. 1).

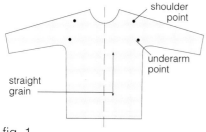

fig. 1

> **NOTE:** The shoulder point is the suggested point for the set-in sleeve and serves as a guide.

• Fold the tracing paper in half and trace the pattern pieces (front and back) onto the tracing paper (Fig. 2).

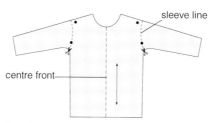

fig. 2

• Decide which finishes you want to use on your tracksuit top. For a top with a twin needle or elastic finishing, for instance, the top and the sleeve must be cut longer than for a top with rib trim.

• Measure the back length and extend the waist to obtain the measured length, if necessary.

• Measure the shoulder length and sleeve length and extend the wrist in order to obtain the measured length, if necessary.

• Decide the type of sleeve you want, and draw in sleeve line (Fig. 2).

• If you want to use colour blocking, draw in the lines (see COLOUR BLOCKING on pages 42–43).

• Mark the straight grain on each pattern piece.

> **NOTE:** The straight grain runs parallel to the centre front, the centre back and the fold on the sleeve (Fig. 14, p. 42).

• Pin pattern pieces onto fabric and mark a 1 cm (⅜ in) seam allowance on the fabric using a marking pen or tailors' chalk and a ruler (Fig. 3).

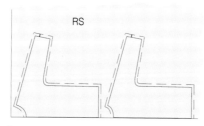

fig. 3

• Mark WS of the fabric with tailors' chalk so that the WS can easily be distinguished from the RS.

• Cut the pattern pieces out of the fabric and stitch together, following the instructions in this chapter.

STITCHING TOGETHER KNITTED FABRICS

Knitted fabrics made on a knitting machine can be cut out and stitched together with the overlocker to make your own jerseys, jackets, coats and cardigans. Steam knitted fabric before stitching it together.

STEAMING KNITTED FABRICS

• Use either a press or a steam iron. Lay knitted fabric flat on ironing board or flat surface.

• To prevent the knitted fabric from being stretched out of proportion during the steaming process, use two elastic bands around the ironing board, moving them according to the width of the piece of fabric. Lay the fabric flat, and move the elastic to its outer edges. Do not stretch knitted fabric. Now pin the outer edges of the knitted fabric to the elastic. If using a flat surface, cover it with a blanket or towel, and pin markers, such as ribbon, onto it.

• Switch on the iron and wait until it begins to steam. Keeping the iron about 1 cm (⅜ in) above the knitted fabric, slowly move it from side to side (Fig. 4), causing the fabric to 'relax'. The knitted fabric now has a much softer appearance, the stitches will not run or unravel when the knitted fabric is cut, and it is easier to handle when it is being stitched together on the overlocker.

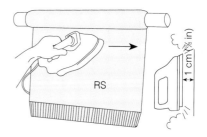

fig. 4

• Roll each piece around a cardboard or plastic tube after steaming, to prevent it from stretching (Fig. 4).

• Leave fabric to stabilize for at least 24 hours before cutting and stitching it. Use same pattern as for tracksuits.

SET-IN OR DROPPED SHOULDER SLEEVE WITH KNITTED FABRIC

REQUIREMENTS
Knitted fabric
Matching industrial wool or
    floss for loopers
Matching polyester cotton
    thread for needles
Hanger or cotton tape
Stitch sealant (see page 23)

SEAM ALLOWANCE
1 cm (⅜ in) should be added

STITCHES
Four-thread overlocking

PATTERNS
Adults: use patterns 1, 2 and 3 on pages 66 and 67
Children: use patterns 4, 5 and 6 on pages 68 and 69

METHOD
1. Fold tracing paper in half and trace patterns onto it. Draw in armhole lines according to shoulder length for set-in or dropped shoulder sleeve. Mark straight grain on front, back and sleeve (Figs. 1 and 2, p. 40).

NOTE: The shoulder point is the suggested point for the set-in sleeve. The other point marked is the suggested underarm point.

2. Cut out pattern pieces and pin onto knitted fabric. Mark 1 cm (⅜ in) seam allowance on fabric using tailors' chalk and cut out (Fig. 3, p. 40). Set differential feed on 2.0 and decrease pressure of pressure foot.

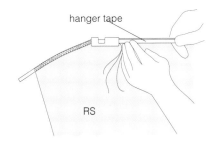

fig. 5

3. Pin shoulder seams together, RS together. Position hanger tape on top of knitted fabric. Stitch from armhole to neck, using four-thread overlocking, while feeding fabric through under pressure foot (Fig. 5). The tape reinforces the shoulder seam and prevents it from waving or stretching.

4. Fold the sleeve in half and mark the centre of the sleeve head with a pin (Fig. 2, p. 44).

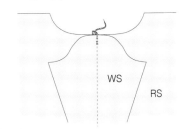

fig. 6

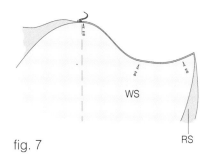

fig. 7

5. Pin the head of the sleeve to the shoulder seam, right sides together (Fig. 6). Position the underarm edges of the sleeve on the underarm edges of the front and back, with right sides and side seam edges together, and pin. Stretch the fabric slightly, if necessary, and insert another pin between the sleeve head and the underarm edge (Fig. 7). Repeat for the other sleeve.

EXAMPLES OF COLOUR BLOCKING AND QUILTING, P. 42–43

6. Stitch the sleeves into the arm-holes using four-thread overlocking, while feeding the knitted fabric through under the pressure foot.

fig. 8a

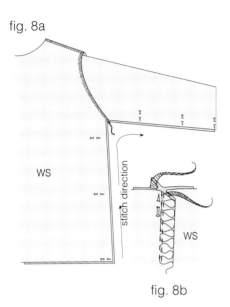

WS

stitch direction

WS

fig. 8b

7. With RS together, pin underarm seams together, matching up arm-hole seams at underarm (Fig. 8b). Using four-thread overlocking, stitch from waist edge to wrist (Fig. 8a) to prevent fabric from stretching. Begin and end stitching on the ribbings by sewing back over your previous stitching (see JOINING ELASTIC TO FORM A CIRCLE, page 12).

8. Use the finish of your choice for the round neck or V-neck.

COLOUR BLOCKING

Colour blocking can be successfully applied to any garment. It will make the garment more interesting and colourful and it also provides the opportunity of using your fabric off-cuts in an economical way. If you follow a few basic rules, it is a very simple technique.

• When colour blocking, trace the pattern piece(s) to be blocked from the graph paper onto the folded tracing paper (Fig. 2, p. 40).
• When blocking the front, do not have a seam across the bust line (for ladies), as this will draw attention to the bust (Fig. 9).

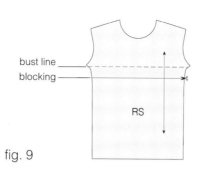

bust line
blocking

RS

fig. 9

• If blocking the front only, use the dropped shoulder sleeve style.
• If diagonally blocking the front, draw first line from shoulder line, starting 3 cm (1¼ in) from neckline for children and 5 cm (2 in) for adults, to side seam at waist (Fig. 10).

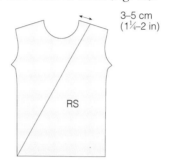

3–5 cm (1¼–2 in)

RS

fig. 10

• Draw more diagonal lines parallel to the first line, or use a second line crossing first line (Fig. 11). For more blocks, draw more horizontal, vertical or parallel lines on front (Fig. 12).

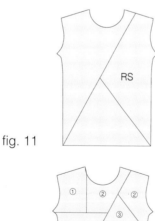

RS

fig. 11

① ② ②
③
③ RS ①
① ②
② ③

fig. 12

• When colour blocking, you should ideally have at least three colours. These may be three colours of fabric,

or two colours of fabric and another of decorative thread applied in a prominent manner (e.g. **flatlocking**). Different shades of the same colour may also be used.

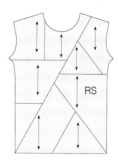

RS

fig. 13

• If you are using **flatlocking** to join the blocks together, be careful not to use too much decorative flatlocking on one garment.
• After tracing the pattern piece onto the folded tracing paper, and drawing in your blocking lines, ensure that the straight grain is marked on all the blocks (Fig. 13). The straight grain runs parallel to the centre front, the centre back and the sleeve fold (Fig. 14).

front   back   sleeve

fig. 14

• Working clockwise, mark blocks according to the colours you want to use, e.g. 1, 2 and 3 (Fig. 12).

RS

fig. 15

• Now cut out the blocks (Fig. 15). Pin the blocks onto the fabric. Mark a 1 cm (⅜ in) seam allowance on the fabric using a marking pen or tailors'

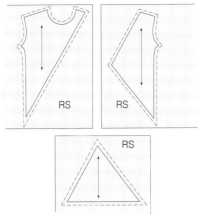

fig. 16

chalk and cut out (Fig. 16). If you do not want a shoulder seam, e.g. for a raglan sleeve, lay the front and back together, joining sleeve seam with transparent adhesive tape (Fig. 17).

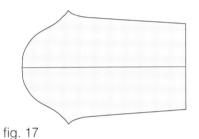

fig. 17

QUILTING

Quilting or decorative stitching may be done either on blocked pieces or on inset pieces.

- Use **three-thread pin-tucks**, **flat-locking** (any variation) or **chain stitch** (any variation – five-thread overlocker only).
- The width of the pin-tucks or flat-locking and the choice of decorative thread depend on size of blocked piece and the type of fabric used.
- Wadding can be used with chain stitch on the five-thread overlocker.
- Remember that pin-tucks or flat-locking will reduce the size of the piece of fabric on which it is used, and that that particular blocked piece or inset piece must be cut larger to allow for the reduction in size. The decorative stitchings are then completed, the blocked piece or inset piece is pinned onto the fabric, the seam allowance is drawn in and the piece is cut out.

SET-IN/DROPPED SHOULDER SLEEVE

BASIC SET-IN/DROPPED SHOULDER SLEEVE

REQUIREMENTS
Stretch fabric
Matching floss and/or polyester cotton thread
Marking tools (see page 23)
Stitch sealant (see page 23)

SEAM ALLOWANCE
1 cm (⅜ in) should be added

STITCHES
Four-thread overlocking (use either three-thread or five-thread over-locking if your overlocker does not have a four-thread facility)

PATTERNS
Adults: use patterns 1, 2 and 3 on pages 66 and 67
Children: use patterns 4, 5 and 6 on pages 68 and 69

METHOD
1. Fold the tracing paper in half and trace the pattern pieces onto it. Draw in the armhole lines according to the shoulder length measured.

NOTE: The shoulder point is the suggested point for the set-in sleeve. The other point marked is the suggested underarm point.

2. Mark straight grain on front, back and sleeve. Cut out pattern pieces. Pin pattern pieces onto fabric. Mark a 1 cm (⅜ in) seam allowance on fabric using tailors' chalk and cut out. Mark WS of fabric with tailors' chalk if not easily distinguishable.

TOPS WITH SET-IN OR DROPPED SHOULDER SLEEVES, P. 43–45

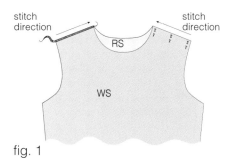

fig. 1

3. Pin shoulder seams together, with right sides together. Stitch from the armhole to the neck (Fig. 1). Press the shoulder seams backwards.

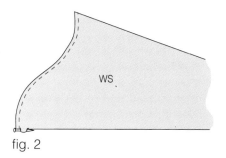

fig. 2

4. Mark centre of sleeve head with a pin (Fig. 2). Pin sleeve head to the shoulder seam, RS together. Position underarm edges of sleeve on underarm edges of front and back, with RS and side seam edges together, and pin. Stretch the fabric slightly, if necessary, and insert another pin between the sleeve head and the underarm edge (Fig. 7, p. 41). Repeat for the other sleeve.

5. Stitch the sleeves into the armholes using four-thread overlocking.

6. With the right sides together, pin the underarm seams together, matching up the armhole seams at the underarm (Fig. 8b, p. 42). Using four-thread overlocking, stitch together from the waist edge to the wrist (Fig. 8a, p. 42).

NOTE: Adjust the differential feed to 1.5 or 2.0 when stitching over the underarm seam, in order to prevent the fabric from bunching where it is too thick.

7. Use the finish of your choice for the neckline, sleeves and waist.

SET-IN OR DROPPED SHOULDER SLEEVE WITH FLATLOCKING

REQUIREMENTS
Stretch fabric
Matching floss and/or polyester cotton thread
Floss or decorative thread
Marking tools (see page 23)
Stitch sealant (see page 23)

SEAM ALLOWANCE
1 cm (⅜ in) should be added

STITCHES

Flatlocking (any variation)
Four-thread overlocking (three- or five-thread if your overlocker does not have a four-thread facility)

PATTERNS

Adults: use patterns 1, 2 and 3 on pages 66 and 67
Children: use patterns 4, 5 and 6 on pages 68 and 69

METHOD

1. Fold tracing paper in half and carefully trace pattern pieces onto it. Draw in armhole lines according to shoulder length measured for set-in or dropped shoulder sleeve.

NOTE: The shoulder point is suggested point for the set-in sleeve. The other point marked is the suggested underarm point.

2. Mark the straight grain on the front, back and sleeve.

3. Cut out the pattern pieces. Pin the pattern pieces onto the fabric. Mark a 1 cm (⅜ in) seam allowance on the fabric using tailors' chalk and cut out. Mark the WS of the fabric with tailors' chalk if WS is not easily distinguishable from RS.

NOTE: The width of the flatlocking you use must be in proportion to the size of the particular garment.

4. Join the blocks of the front together using **flatlocking** (any variation). When using flatlocking on the front, the flatlocking should always face downwards or towards the side seam (Fig. 3).

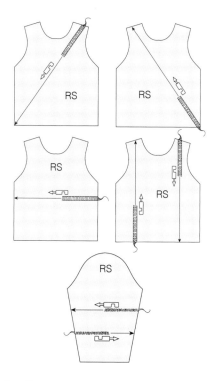

fig. 3

5. Pin shoulder seams, WS together, and stitch using **flatlocking** (any variation). It is important that the flatlocking is stitched in the right direction. As the completed shoulder seam stitching should face backwards, the front is on top while sewing (Fig. 4).

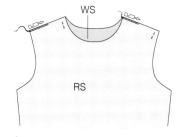

fig. 4

6. Fold the sleeve in half and mark the centre of the sleeve head with a pin (Fig. 2).

7. Pin sleeve head to the shoulder seam, WS together (Fig. 5, p. 45). Position the underarm edges of the

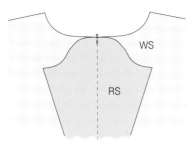

fig. 5

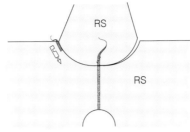

fig. 6

REQUIREMENTS
Stretch fabric
Piping (to make your own piping, see page 11)
Matching floss and/or polyester cotton thread
Floss or decorative thread
Marking tools (see page 23)
Stitch sealant (see page 23)

sleeve on the underarm edges of the front and back, with WS and the side seam edges together, and pin. Stretch the fabric slightly, if necessary, and insert another pin between the sleeve head and the underarm edge (Fig. 7, p. 41). Repeat for the other sleeve.

8. Stitch the sleeves into the armholes using **flatlocking** (any variation). The flatlocking must be stitched in the right direction. As the seam stitching should face towards the sleeve, the sleeve must be at the bottom while sewing (Fig. 6).

9. With RS together, pin underarm seams together, matching up the armhole seams at underarm (Fig. 8b, p. 42). Using four-thread overlocking, stitch together from the waist edge to the wrist (Fig. 8a, p. 42).

> NOTE: Adjust the differential feed to 1.5 or 2.0 when stitching over the underarm seam, in order to prevent the fabric from bunching where it is too thick.

10. Use the finish of your choice for the neckline, sleeves and waist.

SEAM ALLOWANCE
1 cm (⅜ in) should be added

STITCHES
Tape guide attachment, piping foot
Flatlocking (any variation)
Four-thread overlocking (three- or five-thread if your overlocker does not have a four-thread facility)
Zipper foot and straight stitch, stitch length 2–3

PATTERNS
Adults: use patterns 1, 2 and 3 on pages 66 and 67
Children: use patterns 4, 5 and 6 on pages 68 and 69

METHOD
1. Fold the tracing paper in half and trace the pattern pieces onto the folded paper. Draw in the armhole lines according to the shoulder length you have measured.

> NOTE: The shoulder point is suggested point for the set-in sleeve. The other point marked is the suggested underarm point.

2. Use your own design to draw in blocks on front, back and sleeve. Mark the straight grain on the blocks of the front, back and sleeve.

> NOTE: The straight grain runs parallel to the centre front, the centre back and the fold on the sleeve (Fig. 14, p. 42).

BLOCKING WITH FOUR-THREAD OVERLOCKING OR FLATLOCKING

3. Mark the blocks for the different colours. Cut out the pattern pieces.

4. Pin the pattern pieces onto the fabric. Mark a 1 cm (⅜ in) seam allowance on the fabric using tailors' chalk and cut out. Mark the wrong side of the fabric with tailors' chalk if the wrong side is not easily distinguishable from the right side.

5. Join the blocks of the front, the back and the sleeves together using **flatlocking** (any variation), four-thread overlocking or piping. For flatlocking, place the wrong sides together. It is important that the flatlocking is stitched in the right direction (Fig. 3, p. 44). For four-thread overlocking, place the right sides together. If joining the blocks with piping, use tape guide attachment and piping foot on the overlocker.

• ALTERNATIVE: If your overlocker does not have a tape guide attachment and piping foot, stitch the piping to the blocks using the zipper foot and straight stitch on the sewing machine (Fig. 4, p. 36). Finish the raw edges using four-thread overlocking.

6. Pin the shoulder seams together and stitch using **flatlocking** (any variation) or four-thread overlocking. For flatlocking, place the wrong sides together (Fig. 4, p. 44). For four-thread overlocking, place the right sides together (Fig. 1, p. 44). Press shoulder seams backwards.

7. Fold each sleeve in half and mark the centre of the sleeve head with a pin (Fig. 2, p. 44).

8. Pin sleeve head to the shoulder seam. For flatlocking, place the wrong sides together (Fig. 5, p. 45). For four-thread overlocking, place the right sides together. Position the underarm edges of the sleeve on the underarm edges of the front and the back, with the side seam edges together, and then pin (Fig. 6, p. 41). Stretch fabric slightly, if necessary, and insert another pin between the

sleeve head and the underarm edge (Fig. 7, p. 41). Repeat this step to make the other sleeve.

9. Stitch the sleeves into the armholes. For flatlocking, it is important to stitch in the right direction. As the completed seam should face towards the sleeve, the back and the front must be on top while sewing the seam (Fig. 6, p. 45).

10. With the right sides together, pin the underarm seams together, matching armhole seams at the underarm (Fig. 8b, p. 42). Using four-thread overlocking, stitch from waist to wrist (Fig. 8a, p. 42).

> NOTE: Adjust the differential feed to 1.5 or 2.0 when stitching over the underarm seam, in order to prevent the needle from getting stuck in one spot where the fabric is too thick.

11. Use the finish of your choice for the neckline, sleeves and waist.

SET-IN OR DROPPED SHOULDER SLEEVE VARIATIONS

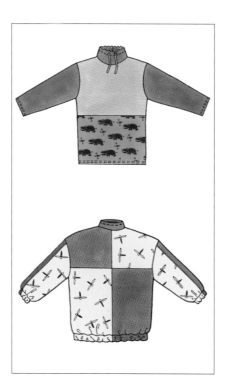

SET-IN OR DROPPED SHOULDER SLEEVE WITH PATCHWORK

REQUIREMENTS

Stretch or non-stretch fabric:
If you are using 3 colours:
1 m (1⅛ yd) of colour 1 (main colour)
50 cm (19½ in) of colour 2
50 cm (19½ in) of colour 3
If you are using 4 colours:
90 cm (1 yd) of colour 1
40 cm (15¾ in) of colour 2
40 cm (15¾ in) of colour 3
40 cm (15¾ in) of colour 4

• OPTIONAL:
40 cm (15¾ in) rib trim

Matching floss and/or polyester cotton thread in the main colour for the overlocker and sewing machine
Rotary cutter (see page 22)
Quilters' ruler (10 cm or 12 cm [4 in or 4¾ in], see page 22)
Marking tools (see page 23)

SEAM ALLOWANCE
1 cm (⅜ in) should be added

STITCHES
Four-thread overlocking (three- or five-thread if your overlocker does not have a four-thread facility)
Straight stitch, stitch length 4–5

PATTERNS
Adults: use patterns 1, 2 and 3 on pages 66 and 67
Children: use patterns 4, 5 and 6 on pages 68 and 69

METHOD
1. Fold tracing paper in half and trace pattern pieces onto it. Draw in the armhole lines according to the shoulder length measured for the set-in or dropped shoulder sleeve.

> NOTE: The shoulder point is the suggested point for the set-in sleeve. The other point marked is the suggested underarm point.

2. Mark straight grain on front, back and sleeve. Cut out pattern pieces.

3. Cut fabric using the rotary cutter and the quilters' ruler: 10 or 12 cm (4 or 4¾ in) strips of 40 or 50 cm (15¾ or 19½ in) each in colours 1, 2 and 3 (and 4, if used).

> **NOTE:** If you are using three colours and the 12 cm (4¾ in) ruler, you need four strips of each colour = 12 strips.
> If you are using three colours and the 10 cm (4 in) ruler, you need five strips of each colour = 15 strips.
> If you are using four colours and the 12 cm (4¾ in) ruler, you need three strips of each colour = 12 strips.
> If you are using four colours and the 10 cm (4 in) ruler, you need four strips of each colour = 16 strips.

4. Mark the wrong side of the strips with a marking pen or tailors' chalk to distinguish the WS from the RS.
• The following methods can be used for patchwork on stretch or non-stretch fabrics. These methods are suitable for tracksuits, jackets and coats – any method may be used for any garment (see JACKETS AND COATS, page 55).

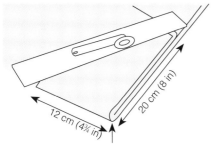

fig. 1

PATCHWORK METHOD 1: FRONT OR BACK

1. Fold fabric 15 cm (6 in) on warp, then 25 cm (10 in) on weft. Using colour 1, cut out a diamond, 20 cm x 12 cm (8 in x 4¾ in), along fold lines (Fig. 1). It will measure 40 cm x 24 cm (15¾ in x 9½ in) (Fig. 2).

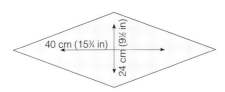

fig. 2

2. Working clockwise, join the strips to the diamond. Pin the first strip to the diamond, with the right sides together, and stitch together using four-thread overlocking (Fig. 3).

> **NOTE:** When joining strips, start the stitching at the short point of the diamond (Fig. 3).

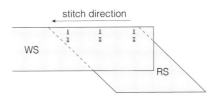

fig. 3

3. Using the sewing machine and straight stitch, top stitch the joined strip on the right side, about 3 mm (⅛ in) from the seam, to hold the overlocking down. The overlocking should always face away from the diamond (Fig. 4).

fig. 4a

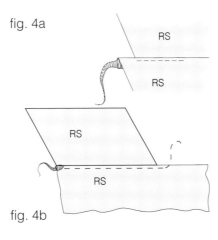

fig. 4b

4. Lay the joined fabric flat and cut away the excess strip on either side of the diamond edge, using a rotary cutter and quilters' ruler (Fig. 5).

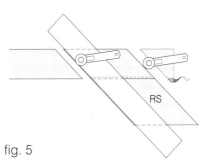

fig. 5

5. Pin next strip to diamond, RS together, and stitch together using four-thread overlocking, starting at the short point of the diamond (Fig. 6).

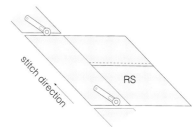

fig. 6

6. Repeat steps 4 and 5. Join two strips in colour 2, then two strips in colour 3, two strips in colour 4 (if you are using four colours), and two strips in colour 1 again.

7. Continue joining fabric strips to the diamond, following step 6, until the patchwork piece is larger than the pattern piece. Lay the pattern piece flat on the patchwork piece and cut away the excess fabric. Remember that no seam allowance has been added to the pattern piece (Fig. 7).

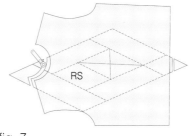

fig. 7

8. Join strips for front until patchwork piece is slightly larger than traced pattern piece all round. Pin pattern piece onto front. Mark 1 cm (⅜ in) seam allowance using tailors' chalk, and cut out (Fig. 8, p. 48).

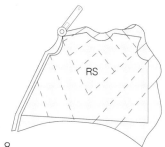

fig. 8

PATCHWORK METHOD 2: BACK – YOKE

1. Join four or five strips, 60 cm (23½ in) long, lengthways to obtain a total width of 50 cm (19½ in), using four-thread overlocking. Using the sewing machine and straight stitch, top stitch on RS 3 mm (⅛ in) from seam to hold the overlocking down. All the overlocking should face in the same direction.

2. Pin the yoke pattern piece diagonally onto the fabric. Mark a 1 cm (⅜ in) seam allowance using tailors' chalk, and cut out the yoke (Fig. 9).

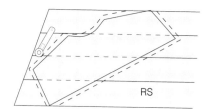

fig. 9

PATCHWORK METHOD 3: BACK – BOTTOM

1. Fold fabric 10 cm (4 in) on warp. Using colour 1, cut out a triangle, 16 cm x 8 cm (6¼ in x 3⅛ in). Opened out, the triangle measures 16 cm x 16 cm (6¼ in x 6¼ in). Pin first strip in colour 2 to the triangle, with RS together, and stitch together using four-thread overlocking.

NOTE: The joined strip must extend beyond the triangle on either side (Fig. 10).

2. Using the sewing machine and straight stitch, top stitch on RS 3 mm (⅛ in) from the seam to hold the overlocking down. It should face away from the triangle (Fig. 10).

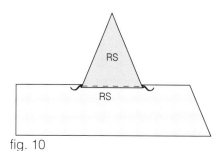

fig. 10

3. Lay the fabric flat and cut away the excess strip on either side of the triangle edge, using a rotary cutter and quilters' ruler (Fig. 11).

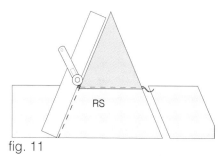

fig. 11

4. Pin the next strip in colour 2 to the other side of the triangle, with RS together, and stitch together using four-thread overlocking.

NOTE: The finished strip must extend beyond the triangle on either side (Fig. 10).

5. Repeat steps 2 and 3. Continue, following steps 4 and 5 with colour 3, then with colour 1, joining strips to either side of triangle, until patchwork piece is larger than pattern piece. Lay pattern piece flat on patchwork piece and cut away any excess fabric. No seam allowance has been added to the pattern piece (Fig. 12).

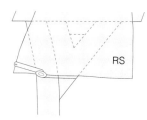

fig. 12

6. Join strips for bottom back until patchwork strips are slightly larger than the traced pattern piece all

round. To complete back, join the bottom back to yoke, RS together, using four-thread overlocking.

PATCHWORK METHOD 4: SLEEVES

1. Join four or five strips of 1–1.2 m (1⅛–1¼ yd) in length together lengthways to obtain a total width of 50 cm (19½ in), using four-thread overlocking. Using the sewing machine and straight stitch, top stitch on the RS 3 mm (⅛ in) from the seam to hold the overlocking down. All the overlocking should face in the same direction.

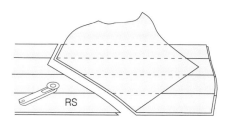

fig. 13

2. Fold fabric and place the sleeve pattern piece diagonally onto fabric, so that the largest part of front of sleeve head is on the fabric (Fig. 13). Cut the rest of the sleeve, i.e. back of sleeve head, out of colour 1 (Fig. 14).

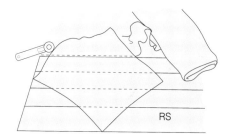

fig. 14

3. Pin the patchwork part of the sleeve to the part cut in colour 1, RS together, and stitch together using four-thread overlocking. Using the sewing machine and straight stitch, top stitch on the RS 3 mm (⅛ in) from the seam to hold the overlocking down. All the overlocking should face in the same direction.

4. Pin the pattern piece for the sleeve onto the fabric. Mark a 1 cm (⅜ in) seam allowance using tailors' chalk, and cut out.

TRACKSUITS WITH PATCHWORK ARE VERY COLOURFUL, P. 46–50

PATCHWORK METHOD 5: SLEEVES

1. Fold fabric 10 cm (4 in) on warp. Using colour 1, cut out a triangle, 20 cm x 12 cm (8 in x 4¾ in). It will measure 24 cm x 20 cm (9½ in x 8 in). Pin first strip in colour 2 to triangle, with RS together, and stitch together using four-thread overlocking.

2. Using the sewing machine and straight stitch, top stitch on RS 3 mm (⅛ in) from seam to hold overlocking down. Overlocking should face away from triangle (Fig. 10, p. 48).

3. Lay fabric flat and cut away the excess strip on either side of triangle edge, using the rotary cutter and quilters' ruler (Fig. 11, p. 48). Pin the next strip in colour 2 to the other side of the triangle, RS together, and stitch using four-thread overlocking.

> NOTE: The finished strip must extend beyond the triangle on either side (Fig. 10, p. 48).

4. Repeat step 3. Continue, following step 4 with colour 3 (colour 4 is optional), then with colour 1, joining fabric strips to either side of triangle. Lay the pattern piece flat on the patchwork piece throughout, cutting away excess fabric.

5. Join strips for the sleeve until the patchwork strips are slightly larger than the pattern piece all round. Pin sleeve pattern piece onto fabric, RS together, and cut out (Fig. 15). Mark a 1 cm seam allowance with tailor's chalk and cut out.

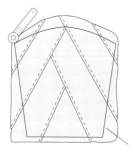

fig. 15   RS

TO COMPLETE

Finish the waist, neck and sleeves of the top according to preference.

RAGLAN SLEEVE

BLOCKING WITH FOUR-THREAD OVERLOCKING, FLATLOCKING OR PIPING

> **REQUIREMENTS**
> Stretch fabric
> Piping (to make your own piping, see page 11)
> Matching floss and/or polyester cotton thread
> Floss or decorative thread
> Marking tools (see page 23)
> Stitch sealant (see page 23)

SEAM ALLOWANCE
1 cm (⅜ in) should be added

STITCHES
Tape guide attachment, piping foot
Flatlocking (any variation)
Four-thread overlocking (three- or five-thread if your overlocker does not have a four-thread facility)
Zipper foot and straight stitch, stitch length 2–3

PATTERNS
Adults: use patterns 1, 2 and 3 on pages 66 and 67
Children: use patterns 4, 5 and 6 on pages 68 and 69

METHOD
1. Fold the tracing paper in half and trace the pattern pieces onto it. Draw in the armhole lines for the raglan sleeve on the front and back.

> NOTE: The shoulder point is the suggested point for the set-in sleeve and serves as a guideline only. The other point marked is the suggested underarm point.

2. Use your own design to draw in blocks on front, back and sleeve. Cut out sleeves. Lay the front and back sleeves together, joining them with adhesive tape (Fig. 17, p. 43).

3. Mark the straight grain on the blocks of the front, back and sleeves.

> NOTE: The straight grain runs parallel to the centre front, the centre back and the sleeve fold.

4. Mark the blocks for the different colours. Cut out the pattern pieces.

5. Pin pattern pieces onto fabric. Mark 1 cm (⅜ in) seam allowance on fabric using tailors' chalk and cut out. Mark WS of fabric with tailors' chalk if not easily distinguishable.

6. Join blocks of the front, back and sleeves together using **flatlocking** (any variation), four-thread overlocking or piping. For flatlocking, place WS together. It is important that the flatlocking is stitched in the right direction (Fig. 3, p. 44). For four-thread overlocking, place right sides together. For piping, use the tape guide attachment and piping foot on the overlocker.

> NOTE: The shorter side of the sleeve is always stitched to the front of the top.

7. Pin sleeves to front and back and stitch together using **flatlocking** (any variation), four-thread overlocking or piping. For flatlocking, place WS together. It is important that the flatlocking is stitched in the right direction. As the completed seam should face towards the sleeve, the back and front must be on top while sewing. For four-thread overlocking, place the RS together and stitch from the underarm to the neck. Attach piping using the tape guide attachment and the piping foot on the overlocker.

• ALTERNATIVE: If your overlocker does not have a tape guide attachment and piping foot, stitch piping to blocks and sleeves using zipper foot and straight stitch on sewing machine (Fig. 4a, p. 36). Pin front and back to sleeves, RS together, and stitch seam along previous stitching, using zipper foot and straight stitch on sewing machine (Fig. 4b, p. 36). Finish raw edges from underarm to neck using four-thread overlocking.

8. With RS together, pin underarm seams together, matching up armhole seams at underarm. Using four-thread overlocking, stitch together from waist to wrist (Fig. 8, p. 42).

NOTE: Adjust the differential feed to 1.5 or 2.0 when stitching over the underarm seam, in order to prevent the fabric from bunching where it is too thick.

9. Use the finish of your choice for the neckline, sleeves and waist.

RAGLAN SLEEVE VARIATIONS

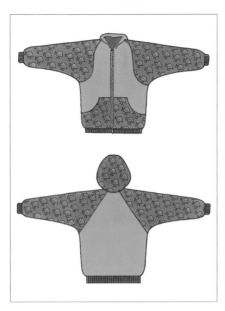

TRACKSUIT TOPS WITH RAGLAN SLEEVES

CUT-ON SLEEVE

CUT-ON SLEEVE WITH FRONT INSET PIECE

REQUIREMENTS
Stretch fabric
Matching floss and/or polyester cotton thread
Floss or decorative thread
Marking tools (see page 23)
Stitch sealant (see page 23)

SEAM ALLOWANCE
1 cm (⅜ in) should be added

STITCHES
Flatlocking (any variation)
Flatlocking with loops
Four-thread overlocking (three- or five-thread if your overlocker does not have a four-thread facility)

PATTERNS
Adults: use patterns 1, 2 and 3 on pages 66 and 67
Children: use patterns 4, 5 and 6 on pages 68 and 69

METHOD
1. Fold tracing paper in half and trace pattern pieces onto it. Draw in lines for inset piece on the front.

2. Mark the straight grain on the inset piece, front and back.

3. Pin the pattern front and back onto fabric. Mark 1 cm (⅜ in) seam allowance on fabric using tailors' chalk and cut out. Mark WS of fabric with tailors' chalk if necessary.

4. Pin the inset piece onto fabric. Remember to cut inset piece larger than pattern piece all round, as flatlocking will reduce size of the piece on which it is used. After decorative flatlocking is completed, the pattern piece is pinned onto inset piece, a 1 cm (⅜ in) seam allowance is added, and it is then cut to the correct size.

5. Using either a marking pen or tailors' chalk, draw the lines for the **flatlocking with loops** (p. 17) on the inset piece. Stitch **flatlocking with loops** all along the lines you have marked.

6. Pin the front to either side of the inset piece, with the wrong sides together, and stitch together using **flatlocking** (any variation).

• ALTERNATIVE: If you feel that enough decorative stitching has been used on the inset piece, pin front to either side of inset piece, RS together, and stitch together using four-thread overlocking.

7. Pin the underarm seams together, with the right sides together, and stitch from the waist edge to the wrist (Fig. 8, p. 42), using four-thread overlocking.

8. Use the finish of your choice for the neckline, sleeves and waist.

CUT-ON SLEEVE WITH BLOCKING AND FLATLOCKING, FOUR-THREAD OVERLOCKING OR PIPING

REQUIREMENTS
Stretch fabric
Piping (to make your own piping, see page 11)
Matching floss and/or polyester cotton thread
Floss or decorative thread
Marking tools (see page 23)
Stitch sealant (see page 23)

SEAM ALLOWANCE
1 cm (⅜ in) should be added

STITCHES
Tape guide attachment, piping foot
Flatlocking (any variation)
Four-thread overlocking (three- or five-thread if your overlocker does not have a four-thread facility)
Zipper foot and straight stitch, stitch length about 2–3

EXAMPLES OF CUT-ON SLEEVES

PATTERNS
Adults: use patterns 1, 2 and 3 on pages 66 and 67
Children: use patterns 4, 5 and 6 on pages 68 and 69

METHOD
1. Fold the tracing paper in half and trace the pattern pieces onto it. Use your own design to draw in blocks on the front, back and sleeve.

2. Mark the straight grain on the front and the back.

NOTE: The straight grain runs parallel to the centre front and the centre back.

3. Mark the blocks for the different colours. Cut out the pattern pieces.

4. Pin the pattern pieces onto the fabric. Mark a 1 cm (⅜ in) seam allowance on the fabric using tailors' chalk and cut out. Mark WS of fabric with tailors' chalk if necessary.

5. Join the blocks of the front and the back together using **flatlocking** (any variation), four-thread overlocking or piping. For flatlocking, place WS together. It is important that the flatlocking is stitched in the right direction (Fig. 3, p. 44). For four-thread overlocking, place RS together. For piping, use tape guide attachment and piping foot.

• ALTERNATIVE: If your overlocker does not have a tape guide attachment and piping foot, attach the piping using the zipper foot and straight stitch on sewing machine (Fig. 4a, p. 36). Pin blocks together with RS together, and stitch seam along previous stitching of piping, using zipper foot and straight stitch, stitch length 2–3, on the sewing machine (Fig. 4b, p. 36). Finish raw edges using four-thread overlocking.

6. Pin the side seams together, with RS together. Stitch from the waist edge to the wrist (Fig. 8, p. 42) using four-thread overlocking.

NOTE: Adjust the differential feed to 1.5 or 2.0 when stitching over the underarm seam, in order to prevent the fabric from bunching where it is too thick.

7. Use the finish of your choice to complete the neckline, the waist and the sleeves.

CUT-ON SLEEVE VARIATIONS

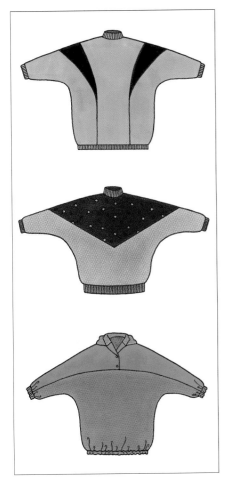

REVERSIBLE TRACKSUITS

SEAM ALLOWANCE
1 cm (⅜ in) should be added

STITCHES
Flatlocking (any variation)
Four-thread overlocking (three- or five-thread if your overlocker does not have a four-thread facility)
Straight stitch, stitch length 3–4

PATTERNS
Adults: use patterns 1, 2 and 3 on pages 66 and 67
Children: use patterns 4, 5 and 6 on pages 68 and 69

REVERSIBLE TRACKSUITS ARE IDEAL FOR CHILDREN

METHOD

1. Fold the tracing paper in half and trace the pattern pieces onto it. Draw in armhole lines according to shoulder length measured. Mark the straight grain on the front, the back and the sleeve. Cut out the pattern pieces. Pin the pattern pieces onto the fabric. Mark a 1 cm (⅜ in) seam allowance on the fabric using tailors' chalk and cut out.

2. Stitch the first and second tops together as in BASIC SET-IN OR DROPPED SHOULDER SLEEVE (see page 43) or SET-IN OR DROPPED SHOULDER SLEEVE WITH FLAT-LOCKING (see page 44). Leave an opening of about 10–15 cm (4–6 in) in the sleeve seam of the first top for turning the top right side out.

3. Finish the round neck, sleeves and waist with rib trim. Stitch rib trim to the first top using the sewing machine and straight stitch. Insert the second top into the first top, RS together, and stitch neck and waist to first top at rib trim using four-thread overlocking.

4. Pull sleeves through to the WS. Keeping underarm seams together, ensure that sleeves of the first and second top are straight, not twisted. Fold sleeve of first top over 5–8 cm (2–3¼ in). Place sleeve of second top over sleeve of first top, and stitch together using four-thread overlocking (Fig. 5, p. 63). Repeat for other sleeve.

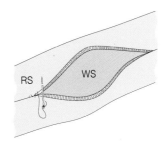

fig. 1

5. Turn the top right side out through the opening in the sleeve. Use neat slip-stitches to close the opening by hand (Fig. 1).

JACKETS
AND COATS

The basic pattern given for a tracksuit top is lengthened and used for making all the jackets and coats in this book. The length of the coat or jacket is determined by the back length, and depends on personal taste, keeping in mind prevailing fashion trends.

Jackets and coats can be made with or without using wadding or a lining. Use wadding if you prefer a warmer coat or jacket, as this will help to keep out the winter cold. Use any of the tracksuit styles given, with blocking if preferred, and choose either set-in, dropped shoulder, raglan or cut-on sleeves.

JACKET OR COAT WITH PIPING OR FLATLOCKING

REQUIREMENTS
Stretch or non-stretch fabric for the jacket
Stretch or non-stretch fabric for lining (optional)
Wadding (optional)
Piping (optional)
Matching floss and/or polyester cotton thread
Floss or decorative thread
Marking tools (see page 23)
Stitch sealant (see page 23)
Fasteners of your choice

SEAM ALLOWANCE
1 cm (⅜ in) should be added

STITCHES
Tape guide attachment, piping foot
Flatlocking (any variation)
Three-thread/three-thread wide overlocking with floss/decorative thread
Four-thread overlocking (three- or five-thread if your overlocker does not have a four-thread facility)

PATTERNS
Adults: use patterns 1, 2 and 3 on pages 66 and 67
Children: use patterns 4, 5 and 6 on pages 68 and 69

METHOD
1. Fold tracing paper in half and trace pattern pieces onto it. Measure the back length, and adjust pattern according to measured length. Draw in armhole lines of your choice.

NOTE: The shoulder point is suggested point for the set-in sleeve and serves as a guideline.

2. Draw in the blocks on the front, or cut each pattern piece out of a different coloured fabric. Mark the straight grain using tailor's chalk.

3. Cut out pattern pieces or blocks, mark 1 cm (⅜ in) seam allowance and cut out. Cut front, back and sleeve out of lining and/or wadding, if using.

4. If using blocking, join the blocks of the front, back and sleeves before stitching the garment together. Join the blocks using **flatlocking**, piping or four-thread overlocking (see the instructions for tracksuits according to the type of finish and the style of sleeve).

• OPTIONAL: If using lining and/or wadding, pin wadding to lining and stitch with three-thread overlocking, stitch length 3–3½, differential feed 1.5. Keep wadding on top and sew.

5. Complete by stitching shoulder seams, sleeves and underarm seams together (see instructions for tracksuits according to style of sleeve).

6. To finish the sleeves, fronts and hem edges, stitch using three-thread or three-thread wide overlocking with floss or decorative thread in the same colour as the flatlocking, or use two different colours, represented in the fabric, in the loopers.

• OPTIONAL: If using lining and/or wadding, place WS of the lining and jacket together and stitch sleeves, fronts and hem edges together. These may also be finished with bias binding in the same colour as the flatlocking, or in a contrasting colour, using either the bias binder on the overlocker (p. 10), or the binding foot on the sewing machine (p. 23) if you do not have a five-thread overlocker.

7. Secure the thread ends with stitch sealant. Complete by attaching the fasteners of your choice.

A COMFORTABLE, EASY-TO-MAKE JACKET FOR ANY OCCASION

CARDIGAN

SEAM ALLOWANCE
A 1 cm (⅜ in) seam allowance has
been included

STITCHES
Tape guide attachment, piping foot
Flatlocking (any variation)
Three-thread or three-thread wide
overlocking with decorative thread
Four-thread overlocking (three- or
five-thread if your overlocker does
not have a four-thread facility)
Straight stitch, stitch length 4–5

PATTERNS
Ladies: use patterns 23, 24 and 25
on pages 84–86
Men: use patterns 26, 27 and 28 on
pages 87–89

METHOD
• OPTIONAL: If you are going to
use knitted fabric for the cardigan,
follow the instructions on page 40
in order to steam the fabric before
stitching it together. Use the same
pattern and method as for tracksuits
when stitching together knitted fabric. Remember also to adjust your
differential feed to 2.0 to prevent
the knitted fabric from waving or
stretching while you sew.

1. Trace the pattern pieces for the
cardigan onto tracing paper.

2. Measure the back length in order
to determine the length of the cardigan, and then adjust the pattern
according to the back measurement.

3. Cut the pattern pieces for the
cardigan out of the fabric.

4. Pin the sleeves to the front, with
right sides together, and stitch using
four-thread overlocking.

> NOTE: The shorter side of the
> sleeve is always the side which
> is stitched to the front.

5. Pin the sleeves to the back, with
the right sides together, and stitch
together using four-thread overlocking. Alternatively, stitch sleeves
together using the tape guide attachment and piping foot. **Flatlocking**
(any variation) may also be used to
stitch the sleeves to the front and
back of the cardigan. Pin the wrong
sides of the sleeves to the front and
the back of the cardigan and stitch
together using the overlocker and
flatlocking (any variation).

6. With the right sides together, pin
the underarm seams together,
matching up the armhole seams at
the underarm. Using four-thread
overlocking, stitch the seams together from the waist edge to the
wrist (Fig. 8, p. 42).

> NOTE: Adjust the differential
> feed to 1.5 or 2.0 when stitching
> over the underarm seam, in
> order to prevent the needle
> from getting stuck in one spot
> where the fabric is too thick.

FOR FABRIC
7. To determine the length of the rib
trim for the waist:
Adults: hip measurement minus
20 cm (8 in);
Children: hip measurement minus
10 cm (4 in).

8. The width of the rib trim for the
waist is 18 cm (7 in) for adults. The
width of the rib trim for the waist is
12 cm (4¾ in) for children.

9. Fold the rib trim in half and
quarter pin mark (p. 12).

10. **Quarter pin mark** the waist of
the cardigan (p. 12).

11. Pin the rib trim to the cardigan,
matching up the pin marks. Stitch
together, using four-thread overlocking and keeping the rib trim on
top (Fig. 3, p. 26).

12. To determine the length of the
rib trim for the neck, place the
shoulder seams together and lay the
cardigan flat. Measure the back of
the neck, positioning the tape
measure on its side (Fig. 1). Multiply
this measurement by two to determine the total back neck measurement. Measure two-thirds of the
back neck measurement on the rib
trim. Now measure the front of the
cardigan down to the hemline,
including the rib trim (Fig. 1). Multiply this measurement by two and
deduct 10 cm (4 in) for the final
front measurement. Add this to the
back neck measurement to determine the total length of the rib trim.
The width of the rib trim for the
neck is 12 cm (4¾ in).

fig. 1

13. Fold the rib trim in half lengthways, with RS together, and stitch
up short ends of the rib trim using
four-thread overlocking (Fig. 2).
Trim the corners diagonally, cutting
away excess fabric, and turn RS out.

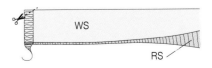

fig. 2a

FOR KNITTED FABRIC

14. To determine the length of the rib trim for the neck, place the shoulder seams together and lay the cardigan flat. Measure the back neck and the front opening, positioning the tape measure on its side. Multiply this measurement by two and deduct 10 cm (4 in) to determine the total measurement. The width of the rib trim is 12–16 cm (4¾–6½ in).

15. Fold the rib trim in half lengthways, with right sides together, and stitch up the short ends of the rib trim using four-thread overlocking (Fig. 2b). Trim the corners diagonally, cutting away any excess fabric, and turn right side out.

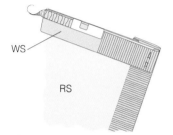

fig. 2b

• OPTIONAL: For knitted fabric one edge only may be stitched to the fabric, right sides together, using four-thread overlocking. Fold over to wrong side and sew to wrong side by hand, using long tacking stitches, or use the sewing machine and straight stitch, stitch length 4–5.

16. Secure the thread ends with stitch sealant to prevent fraying.

17. Complete sleeve according to preference, see page 36.

18. Finish the cardigan, attaching buttons or poppers to the rib trim.

NOTE: Buttonholes are prone to stretching when they are made on rib trim. This can be prevented by stitching buttonholes over a piece of embroidery or crochet thread, or otherwise by placing paper at the back and stitching on the paper.

RAINCOAT

This easy, loose-fitting coat is cut to measure, using a block pattern. The pattern is ideal for a raincoat and can also be used for a coat, dressing gown or bed jacket.

REQUIREMENTS
Raincoat fabric with a special plastic coating
Non-stretch plain fabric for bias binding
Matching floss and/or polyester cotton thread
Floss or decorative thread
Marking tools (see page 23)
Stitch sealant (see page 23)

SEAM ALLOWANCE
1 cm (⅜ in) should be added

STITCHES
Chain stitch with bias binder
Ladder stitch with floss or decorative thread
Three-thread wide overlocking with floss or decorative thread
Four-thread overlocking (three- or five-thread if your overlocker does not have a four-thread facility)
Straight stitch, stitch length 4–5

PATTERNS
For all sizes: design your own pattern following the instructions.

METHOD
• OPTIONAL: For a hood, use pattern 6 on page 69 for children and pattern 3 on page 67 for adults.

TO DETERMINE THE AMOUNT OF FABRIC
1. To determine length of the coat, measure down back to the desired length, A to B plus hem. Also measure sleeve length, A to C plus hem (Fig. 1). Add these two measurements together to obtain length of fabric you need (e.g. A to B = 90 cm [35½ in] and A to C = 35 cm [13¾ in]; 90 cm + 35 cm = 125 cm [35½ in + 13¾ in = 49¼ in]; 125 cm [49¼ in]

plus hem = total length). Join the fabric if it is narrower than your hip measurement. The raincoat must be slightly loose-fitting.

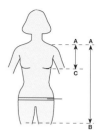

fig. 1

TO DESIGN AND CUT YOUR OWN PATTERN

NOTE: First practise on a piece of paper before cutting fabric.

fig. 2

2. Cut fabric to length measured in step 1. Lay flat and fold top edge over widthways, the length of the sleeve, towards you. Pin down (Fig. 2).

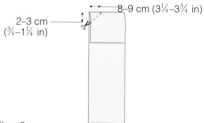

fig. 3

3. Fold fabric in half lengthways and cut out back of the neck, through all the layers (Fig. 3). The depth of the neck is 2–3 cm (¾–1¼ in).

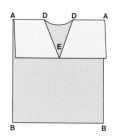

fig. 4

4. Unfold fabric and cut open diagonally from neck, D, to centre front, E (Fig. 4, p. 58). Fold the two outer edges, A and B, inwards (towards centre back). Cut open front only, in line with bottom edge of sleeve, F. Do not cut the back (Fig. 5).

fig. 5

5. Unfold the fabric. The cutting is now completed (Fig. 6).

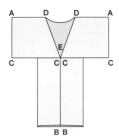

fig. 6

• OPTIONAL: Do not cut the front neck diagonally, otherwise a hood cannot be attached.

6. With RS together, pin the seam on the front together, and stitch using **wide ladder stitch with floss or decorative thread** (p. 18).

• OPTIONAL: Cut the sleeve bands 10–12 cm (4–4¾ in) wide. Fold bands in half, WS together, and pin to WS of fabric. Stitch together using **flatlocking** (any variation). The completed sleeve must equal the measured sleeve length.

7. Make your own bias binding (p. 11). Stitch the bias binding to the sleeve edges, neck and front using **bias binder with chain stitch** (p. 10) on the overlocker.

NOTE: If you do not have a five-thread overlocker, attach binding using the binding foot on the sewing machine (p. 23).

THIS CHEERFUL RAINCOAT WILL BRIGHTEN THE GREYEST DAY

• OPTIONAL: If you are making a hood, stitch the hood seam using **wide ladder stitch with floss or decorative thread** (p. 18). Stitch bias binding to the face edge of the hood using **bias binder with chain stitch** (p. 10) on the overlocker. Pin the hood to the neck edge, with the right sides together, and stitch using four-thread overlocking.

8. Cut the front and the neck band 10–12 cm (4–4¾ in) wide. Fold the strip in half, with the wrong sides together, and pin to the wrong side of the front and neck.

9. With RS together, pin the underarm seams together and stitch from the hem edge to the wrist, using four-thread overlocking.

10. Stitch the bias binding to the hem edge of the raincoat using **bias binder with chain stitch** (p. 10) on the overlocker.

• OPTIONAL: Stitch the hem edge using three-thread wide overlocking with floss or decorative thread.

11. Secure the thread ends with stitch sealant to prevent fraying.

EASY COAT FOR LADIES

SEAM ALLOWANCE
1 cm (⅜ in) has been included

STITCHES
Three-thread or three-thread wide
overlocking with decorative thread
Four-thread overlocking (three- or
five-thread if your machine does not
have a four-thread facility)
Straight stitch, stitch length 2–3

PATTERNS
Ladies: use patterns 29, 30, 31 and
32 on pages 90–93 for all sizes

METHOD
1. Trace the pattern pieces for the
coat onto tracing paper.

2. Cut out of the fabric: back (on
the fold), 2 x fronts, 2 x sleeves
and 4 x pockets.

3. Pin pockets to side seams of the
front and back, RS together, and
stitch using four-thread overlocking.

4. With RS together, pin and stitch
the collar seam onto the front of the
coat using four-thread overlocking.

5. With the right sides together, pin
and stitch the collar on the front to
the back of the neck, using four-
thread overlocking.

6. Clip the fabric at the corners on
the front (Fig. 1). Stitch, keeping the
back on top and holding the fabric
straight while you sew.

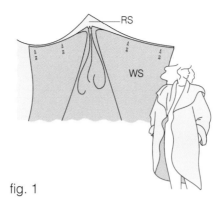

fig. 1

7. Fold the sleeve in half and mark
the centre of the sleeve head with a
pin. Repeat for the other sleeve.

8. Pin the sleeve head to the shoulder seam, with right sides together.
Position the underarm edges of the
sleeve on the underarm edges of the
front and back, with right sides and
side seam edges together, and pin.
Repeat for the other sleeve.

9. Stitch the sleeves into the armholes using four-thread overlocking.

10. With the right sides together, pin
the underarm seams together,
matching up the armhole seams at
the underarm. Align the pockets,
which must also be together. Using
four-thread overlocking, stitch sides
together from the hem edge, around
the pocket to the wrist.

11. To reinforce the pocket, stitch
up the pocket from its bottom edge
to approximately 5 cm (2 in) from
the edge, using the sewing machine
and straight stitch.

12. Finish the sleeve edges, the collar edges and the hem edges using
three-thread wide overlocking.

NOTE: Either floss or decorative
thread may be used in one or
both of the loopers.

• OPTIONAL: You can either use
floss or decorative thread of two different colours, or otherwise two
shades of the same colour thread in
the loopers of the overlocker.

REVERSIBLE JACKET WITH HOOD OR COLLAR

SEAM ALLOWANCE
1 cm (⅜ in) has been included

STITCHES
Tape guide attachment, piping foot
Flatlocking (any variation)
Four-thread overlocking (three- or
five-thread, if your overlocker does
not have a four-thread facility)
Straight stitch, stitch length 2–3

THESE REVERSIBLE JACKETS WILL DELIGHT EACH MEMBER OF THE FAMILY

PATTERNS

Adults: use patterns 13, 14, 15, 16 and 17 on pages 76–79

Children: use patterns 18, 19, 20, 21 and 22 on pages 80–83

METHOD

1. Trace the pattern pieces for the jacket onto tracing paper. Measure the back length to determine the length of the jacket, and adjust the length of the pattern according to the measured length.

2. Mark the straight grain on the front, the back and the sleeve. Pin the pattern pieces onto the fabric.

NOTE: 1 cm (⅜ in) seam allowance has already been added.

PREPARATION

3. Printed fabric is usually used to make the first jacket. For the second jacket, choose three colours represented in the printed fabric. Colours 1 and 2 are for the Quantec/polyester cotton and colour 3 is for the piping/flatlocking and zipper. Alternatively, you may use colour 1 for Quantec/polyester cotton or denim and colours 2 and 3 for the piping/flatlocking and zipper.

4. Cut pattern pieces out of printed fabric for the first jacket: back (on fold), 2 x fronts, 2 x sleeves, 2 x hoods (optional) and 2 x pockets. (There is no pattern for the collar.)

5. Cut the pattern pieces out of the fabric for the second jacket: back (on fold), 2 x fronts, 2 x sleeves, 2 x hoods (optional) and 2 x pockets.

6. Cut out of wadding: back (on fold), 2 x fronts, 2 x sleeves and 2 x hoods (optional).

7. Pin the wadding to the WS of each piece of the first jacket.

8. With the wadding on top, stitch together using three-thread overlocking, stitch length 3–3½ and differential feed 1.5.

PIPING

9. With RS together, pin the fronts to the backs and stitch using the tape guide attachment and piping foot on the overlocker.

• If you want top stitching, stitch two rows using sewing machine and straight stitch, stitch length 4–5. Shoulder seams should face towards the front for adults (Fig. 1a) and the back for children (Fig. 1b).

• With RS together, pin the sleeves to the jacket and stitch using the tape guide attachment and piping foot on the overlocker.

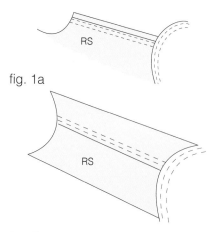

fig. 1a

fig. 1b

• ALTERNATIVE: If your overlocker does not have a tape guide attachment and piping foot, stitch piping to the front shoulder seams and the sleeves using the zipper foot and straight stitch, stitch length 2–3, on the sewing machine (Fig. 4, p. 36).

• If you want top stitching, stitch two rows using the sewing machine and straight stitch, stitch length 4–5. The seam should face towards the sleeve (Fig. 1).

FLATLOCKING

9. With wrong sides together, pin the fronts and backs together and stitch using **flatlocking** (any variation). Keep the front at the top so that the shoulder seam will lie flat towards the back.

• With WS together, pin the sleeves to the jacket and stitch using **flatlocking** (any variation). Keep the sleeve at the bottom.

PIPING AND FLATLOCKING

10. With RS together, pin the underarm seams together, matching up the armhole seams at the underarm. Using four-thread overlocking, stitch together from the waist edge to the wrist (Fig. 8, p. 42).

NOTE: Adjust the differential feed to 1.5 or 2.0 when stitching over the underarm seam, in order to prevent the needle from getting stuck in one spot where the fabric is too thick.

STITCHING UP THE FIRST JACKET (PRINTED FABRIC)

11. Using the tape guide attachment and piping foot on the overlocker, stitch the shoulder seams and armholes with piping (without any top stitching, as the jacket is too thick due to the wadding), or use **flatlocking** (any variation).

12. With RS together, pin underarm seams together, matching up armhole seams at underarm. Using four-thread overlocking, stitch together from the waist edge to the wrist. Leave an opening of 15 cm (6 in) in the underarm seam of one sleeve for turning jacket RS out (Fig. 2).

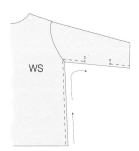

fig. 2

FINISHING THE JACKETS (HOOD OPTIONAL)

PIPING

13. Using the tape guide attachment and piping foot on the overlocker, stitch piping to the hood seams of the first and second jackets. Using the tape guide attachment and the piping foot on the overlocker, stitch the piping to the face edge of the hood for the first jacket.

• ALTERNATIVE: If your overlocker does not have a tape guide attachment and piping foot, attach piping using zipper foot and straight stitch, stitch length 2–3, on sewing machine.

FLATLOCKING
13. With WS together, stitch hood seams of first and second jackets using **flatlocking** (any variation).
• Using the sewing machine, make a vertical buttonhole on the hood of the first jacket, 3 cm (1¼ in) from the neck edge and 1.5 cm (⅝ in) from the face edge, 2 cm (¾ in) in length (Fig. 3, p. 35).
• Pin the hoods together. To make a casing for the cord, stitch 3 cm (1¼ in) from the face edge using the sewing machine and straight stitch, stitch length 3–4.

COLLAR (OPTIONAL)
14. Place shoulder seams together and lay jacket flat. Measure the neck, positioning tape measure on its side. Multiply this measurement by two to determine total neck measurement. Cut collar to length of neck measurement. The width of the collar is 15 cm (6 in). Cut one collar for each jacket, and one out of wadding.

15. Stitch the wadding to the collar of the first jacket all round.

16. Pin collars of first and second jackets together and stitch two short ends and one long end together, RS together. Trim away excess fabric at the corners and turn to the RS.

17. Top stitch two short ends and one long end 1 cm (⅝ in) from the edge, using the sewing machine and straight stitch, stitch length 3–4.

POCKETS
18. Stitch piping to pocket (Fig. 5, p. 38). To attach piping at an outside corner, see p. 11.

19. Place second pocket (lining) on first pocket, RS together, and stitch together along stitching of piping. Trim away the excess fabric at the corners and turn right side out.

20. Pin pockets to side seams of the second jacket and stitch down as indicated, using sewing machine and straight stitch (Fig. 4, p. 37).

ATTACHING HOOD OR COLLAR AND ZIPPER
21. With RS together, pin hood or collar to the neckline of the second jacket, 1.5 cm (⅝ in) from the centre front on either side.

22. Attach hood or collar, stitching from the centre front to the centre back on either side (Fig. 3).

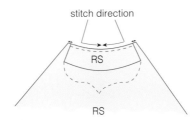

fig. 3

23. With right sides together and the collar or hood on the inside, pin the first jacket to the neckline of the second jacket. Stitch the jackets together at the neckline, along the previous stitching.

24. Pin the zipper to the first jacket and then stitch, using the sewing machine and zipper foot (Fig. 4).

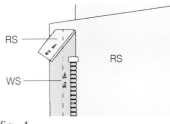

fig. 4

25. Place right sides of the jackets together, and then stitch the second jacket to the first one at the zipper, along the first stitching.

• OPTIONAL: If using poppers, cut four strips of the fabric for the first jacket, the length of jacket and 8 cm (3¼ in) wide. Fold in half lengthways, wrong sides together, and pin two strips one on top of the other to each side of the jacket.

26. Pin bottom ends of the jackets together, right sides together, and stitch using four-thread overlocking.

SLEEVES
27. Pull sleeves through to WS. Keeping underarm seams together, ensure that sleeves of the first and second jackets are straight, and not twisted. Fold over sleeve of second jacket 5–8 cm (2–3¼ in). Place the sleeve of the first jacket over the sleeve of the second jacket (Fig. 5).

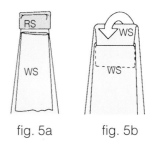

fig. 5a   fig. 5b

28. Pin and stitch sleeves together, using four-thread overlocking. Repeat for the other sleeve.

29. Turn the jackets RS out through the opening in the sleeve. Use slip-stitches to close the opening.

30. Pin and top stitch the bottom edge of the jacket 1 cm (⅜ in) from the bottom edge, using the sewing machine and straight stitch.

31. To make a casing for the cord, stitch above the last top stitching, thus starting directly below the end of the zipper (Fig. 6).

fig. 6

• OPTIONAL: Using the sewing machine and straight stitch, top stitch 1 cm (⅜ in) from zipper and neck up to shoulder seam (Fig. 6).

32. Thread cord through the hood and the bottom edge of the jacket.

PATTERNS

This section contains all the patterns referred to under each project. Every pattern piece is numbered and should be enlarged according to the scale given on that particular page. On full sized graph paper, one square = 1 cm x 1 cm (⅜ in x ⅜ in), or one square = 2 cm x 2 cm (¾ in x ¾ in). Ensure that you enlarge all the pattern pieces accurately – take note of the scale which is given for each pattern piece and enlarge according to this. Follow either the metric or the imperial measurements throughout – do not swap from one to the other.

The following list gives the sizes of the garments. Note that the sizes of the reversible jacket for children are given according to age, not measurement.

TRACKSUIT TOPS (according to chest measurement)
Adults:
Small   80 cm (32 in)
Medium   88 – 92 cm   (34 – 36 in)
Large   97 – 102 cm   (38 – 40 in)
Extra large   107 – 112 cm   (42 – 44 in)

Children:
Small   2 – 4 years   54 – 58 cm (21 – 23 in)
Medium 5 – 8 years   60 – 66 cm (24 – 26 in)
Large   9 – 12 years   68 – 74 cm (27 – 30 in)

TRACKSUIT BOTTOMS/PANTS
(according to waist and hip measurements)

	Waist	Hip
Ladies:		
Small	64 cm (25 in)	89 cm (35 in)
Medium	72 cm (28½ in)	97 cm (38 in)
Large	82 cm (32 in)	107 cm (42 in)
Extra large	92 cm (36 in)	117 cm (46 in)
Men:		
Small	74 cm (30 in)	92 cm (36 in)
Medium	82 cm (32 in)	100 cm (39½ in)
Large	90 cm (36 in)	108 cm (42½ in)
Extra large	102 cm (40 in)	118 cm (46 in)

Children:
Small   54 cm (21 in)   59 cm (23 in)
Medium   59 cm (23 in)   69 cm (27 in)
Large   63 cm (25 in)   79 cm (31 in)

REVERSIBLE JACKETS
Adults (according to chest measurement)
Small   87 – 92 cm   (34 – 36 in)
Medium   97 – 102 cm   (38 – 40 in)
Large   107 – 112 cm   (42 – 44 in)

Children (according to age):
Small   4 years
Medium   6 years
Large   8 years
Extra large   10 years

CARDIGAN (according to chest measurement)
Ladies:
Small   80 – 83 cm   (32 – 32¾ in)
Medium 87 – 92 cm   (34 – 36 in)
Large   97 – 107 cm   (38 – 42 in)

Men:
Small   87 – 92 cm   (34 – 36 in)
Medium 97 – 102 cm   (38 – 40 in)
Large   107 – 112 cm   (42 – 44 in)

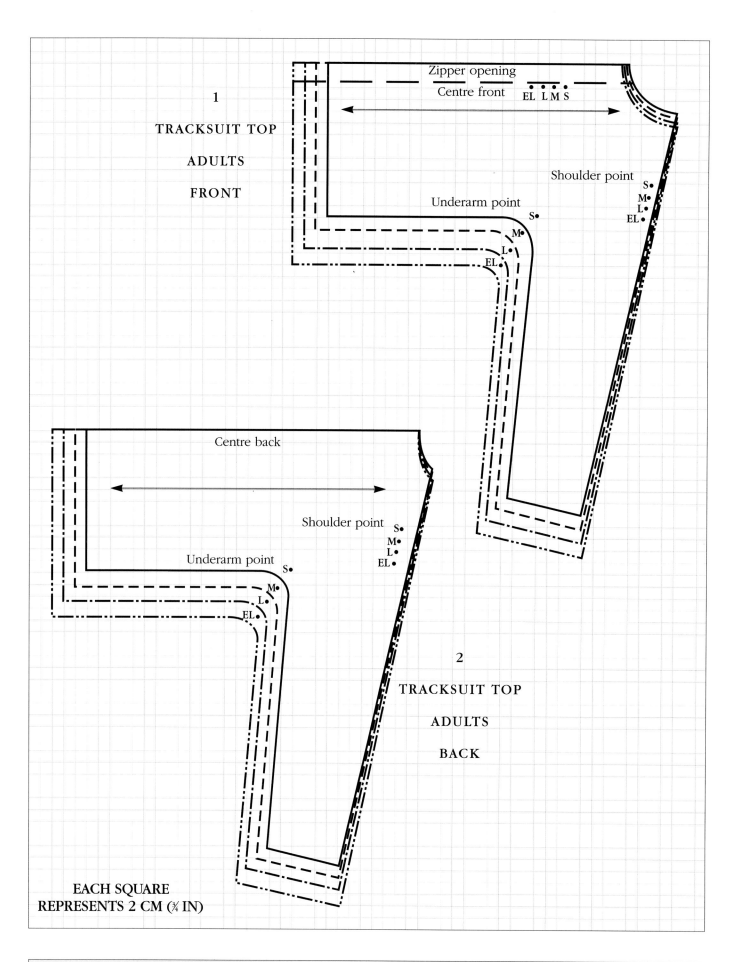

1

TRACKSUIT TOP

ADULTS

FRONT

Zipper opening

Centre front   EL L M S

Shoulder point   S•
                                 M•
                                 L•
                                 EL•

Underarm point   S•
                     M•
                   L•
                 EL•

Centre back

Shoulder point   S•
                M•
                L•
                EL•

Underarm point   S•
                M•
              L•
            EL•

2

TRACKSUIT TOP

ADULTS

BACK

EACH SQUARE
REPRESENTS 2 CM (¾ IN)

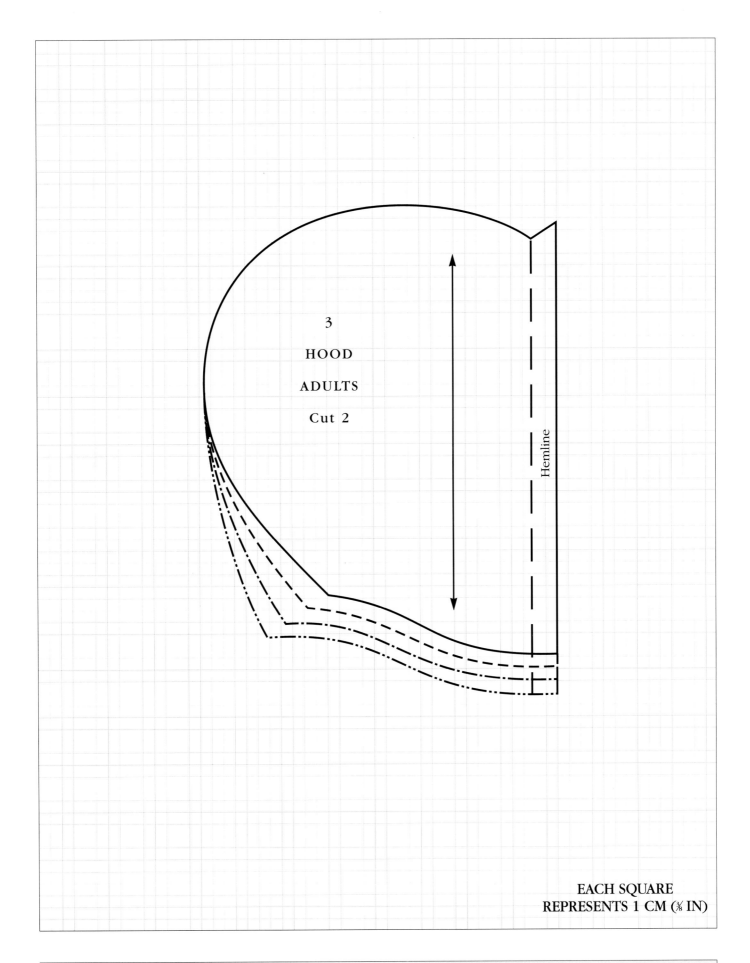

3

HOOD

ADULTS

Cut 2

Hemline

EACH SQUARE
REPRESENTS 1 CM (⅜ IN)

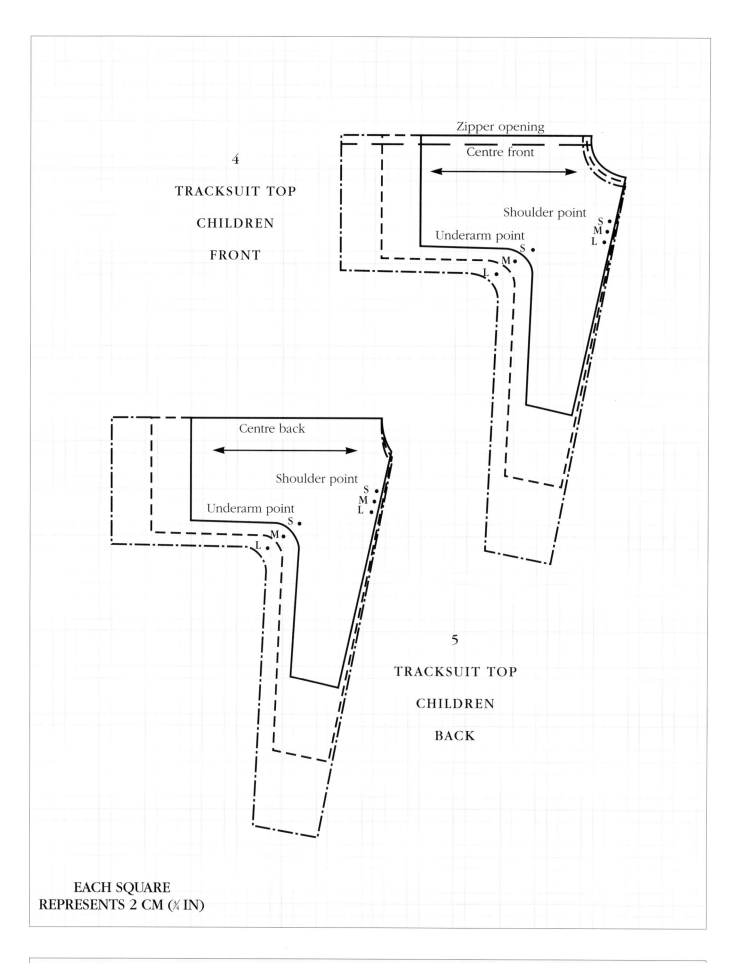

4

TRACKSUIT TOP

CHILDREN

FRONT

Zipper opening

Centre front

Shoulder point

S
M
L

Underarm point

S

M

L

Centre back

Shoulder point

S
M
L

Underarm point

S

M

L

5

TRACKSUIT TOP

CHILDREN

BACK

**EACH SQUARE
REPRESENTS 2 CM (¾ IN)**

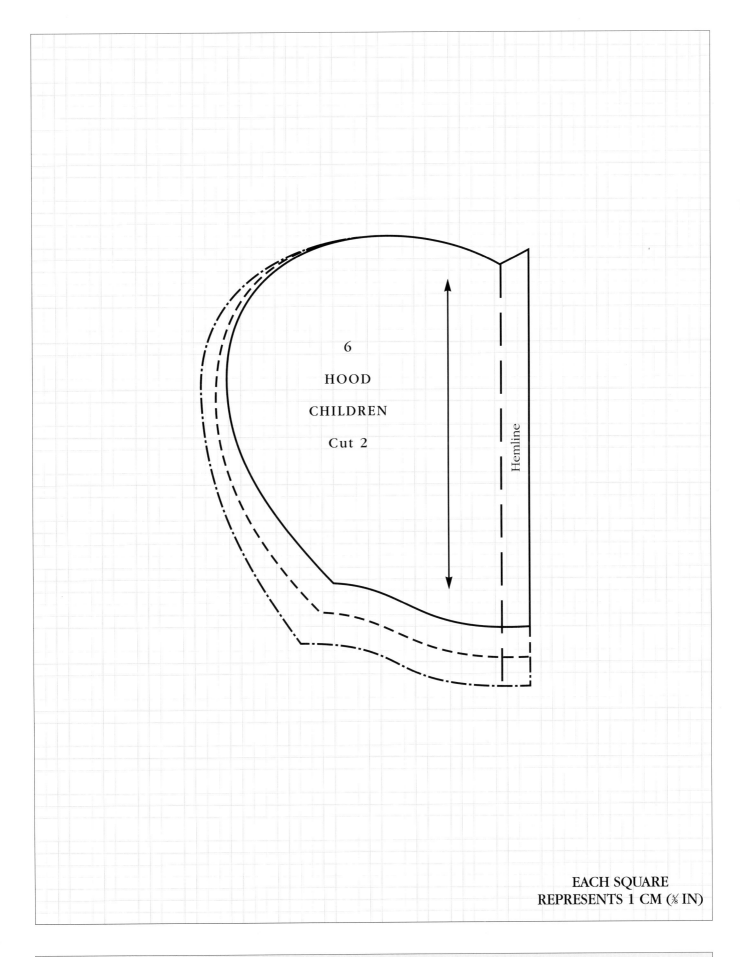

6

HOOD

CHILDREN

Cut 2

Hemline

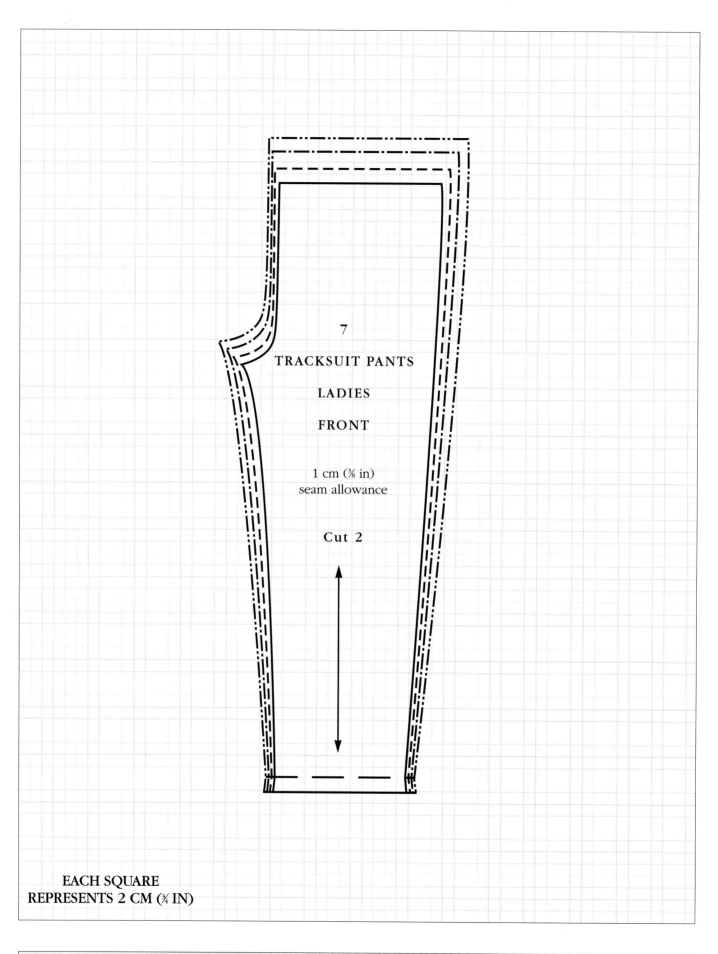

7

TRACKSUIT PANTS

LADIES

FRONT

1 cm (⅜ in)
seam allowance

Cut 2

**EACH SQUARE
REPRESENTS 2 CM (¾ IN)**

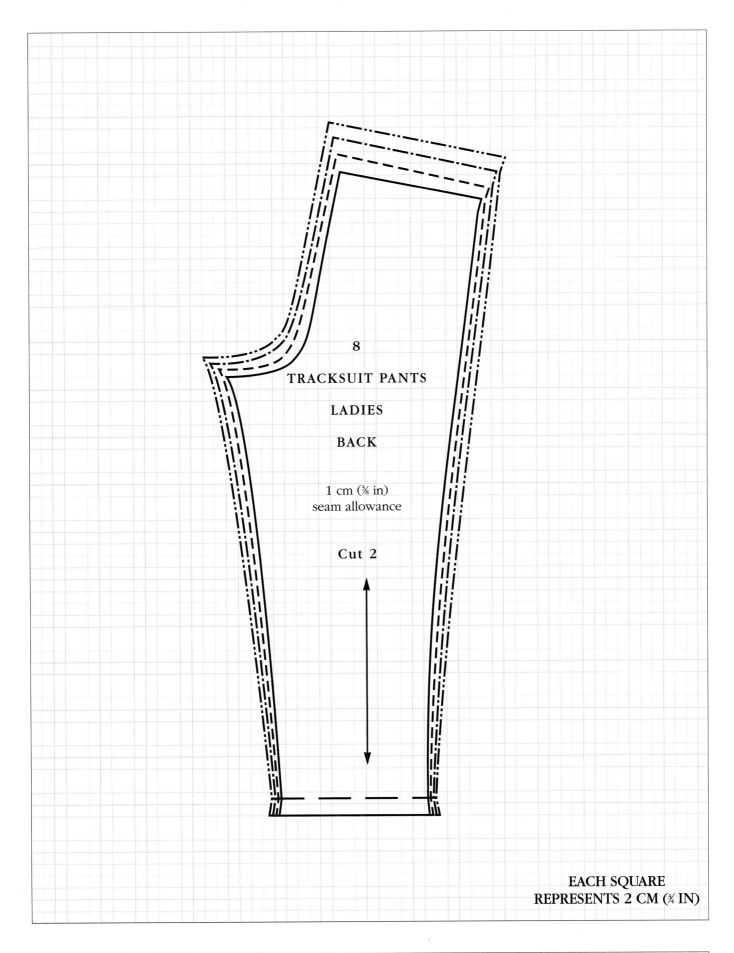

8

TRACKSUIT PANTS

LADIES

BACK

1 cm (⅜ in)
seam allowance

Cut 2

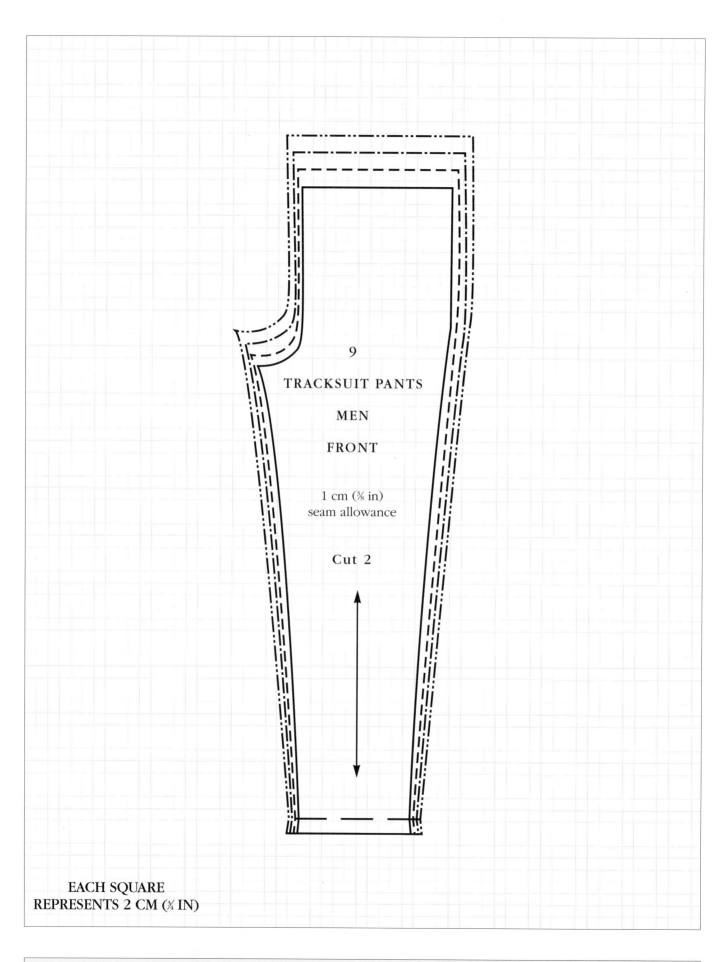

9

TRACKSUIT PANTS

MEN

FRONT

1 cm (⅜ in)
seam allowance

Cut 2

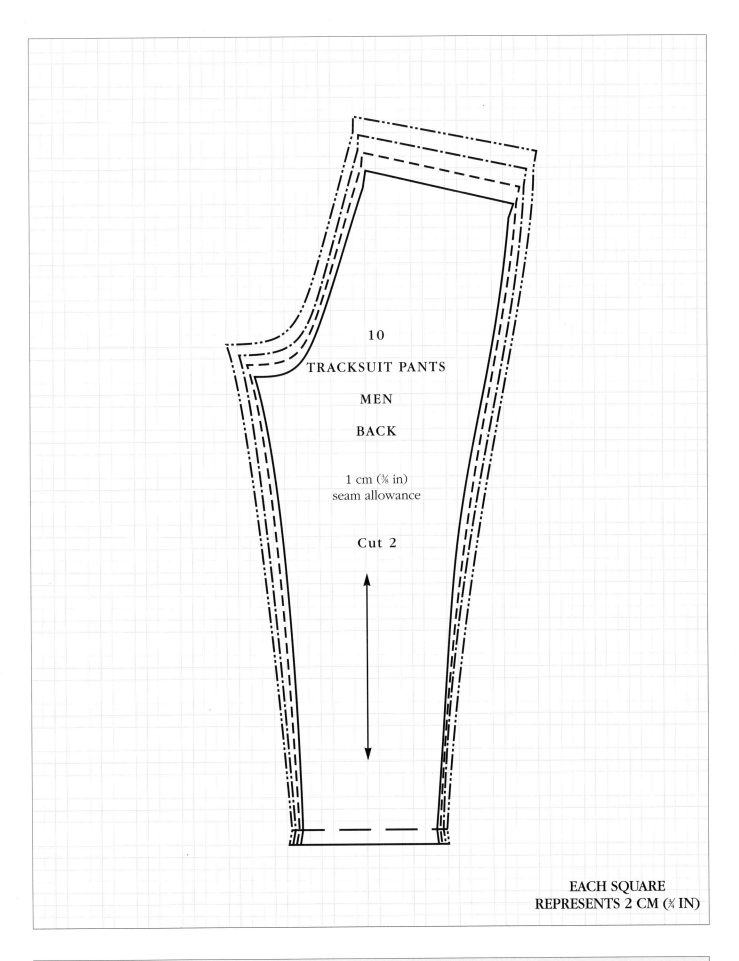

10

TRACKSUIT PANTS

MEN

BACK

1 cm (⅜ in)
seam allowance

Cut 2

**EACH SQUARE
REPRESENTS 2 CM (¾ IN)**

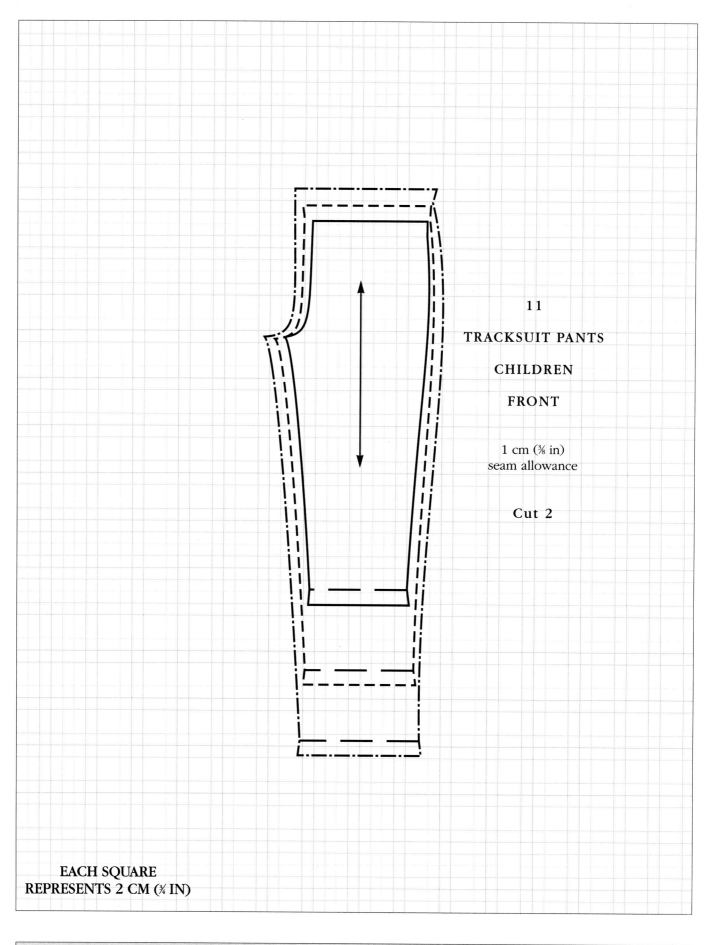

11

TRACKSUIT PANTS

CHILDREN

FRONT

1 cm (⅜ in)
seam allowance

Cut 2

**EACH SQUARE
REPRESENTS 2 CM (¾ IN)**

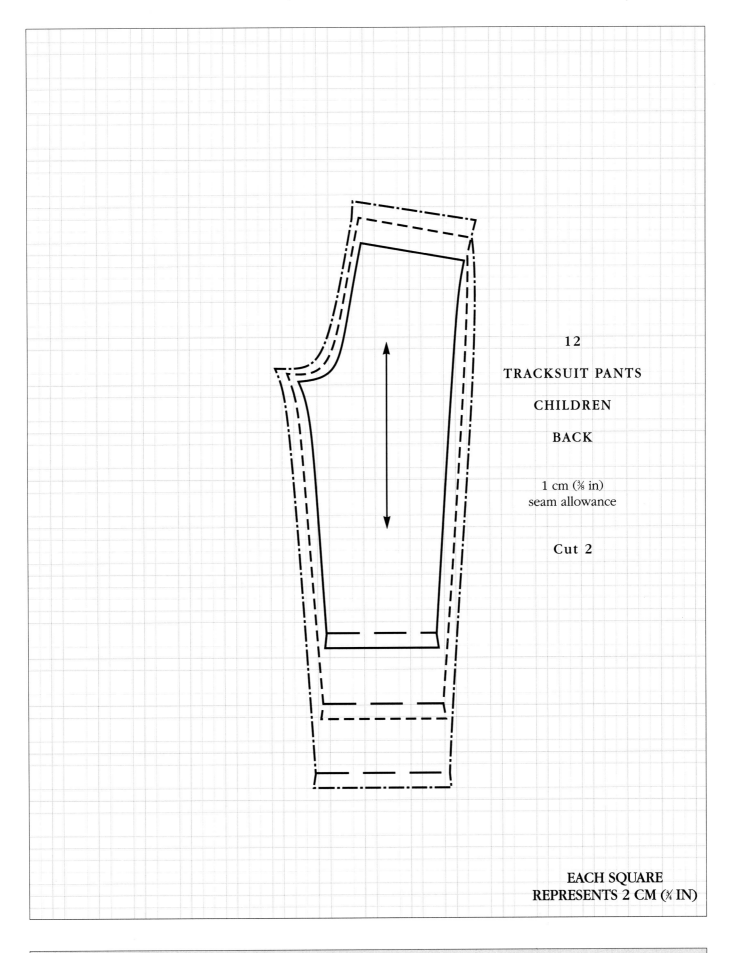

12

TRACKSUIT PANTS

CHILDREN

BACK

1 cm (⅜ in)
seam allowance

Cut 2

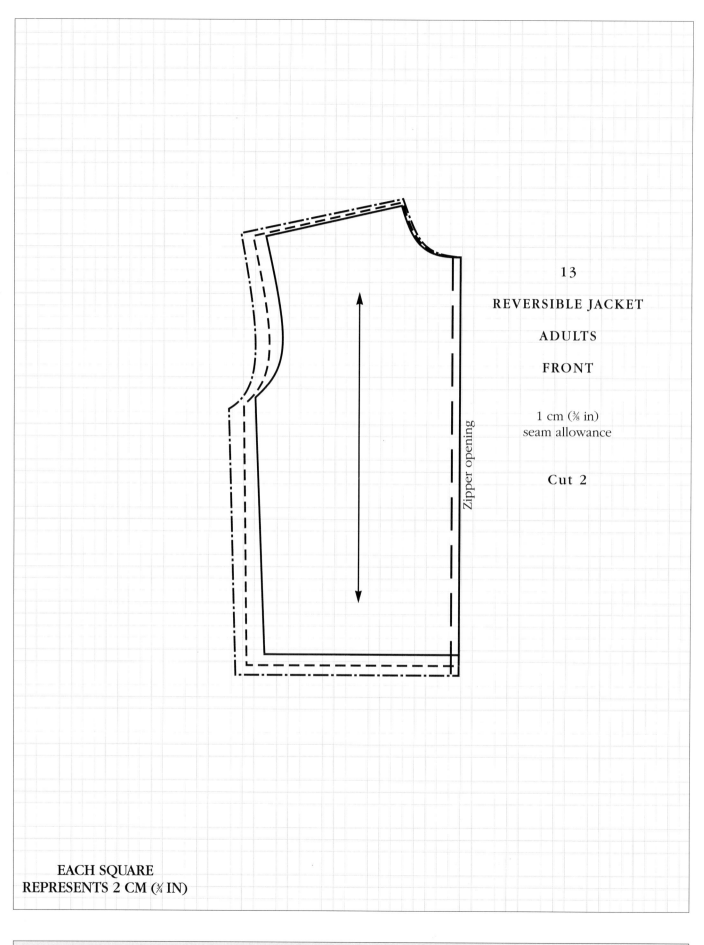

13

REVERSIBLE JACKET

ADULTS

FRONT

1 cm (⅜ in)
seam allowance

Cut 2

Zipper opening

**EACH SQUARE
REPRESENTS 2 CM (¾ IN)**

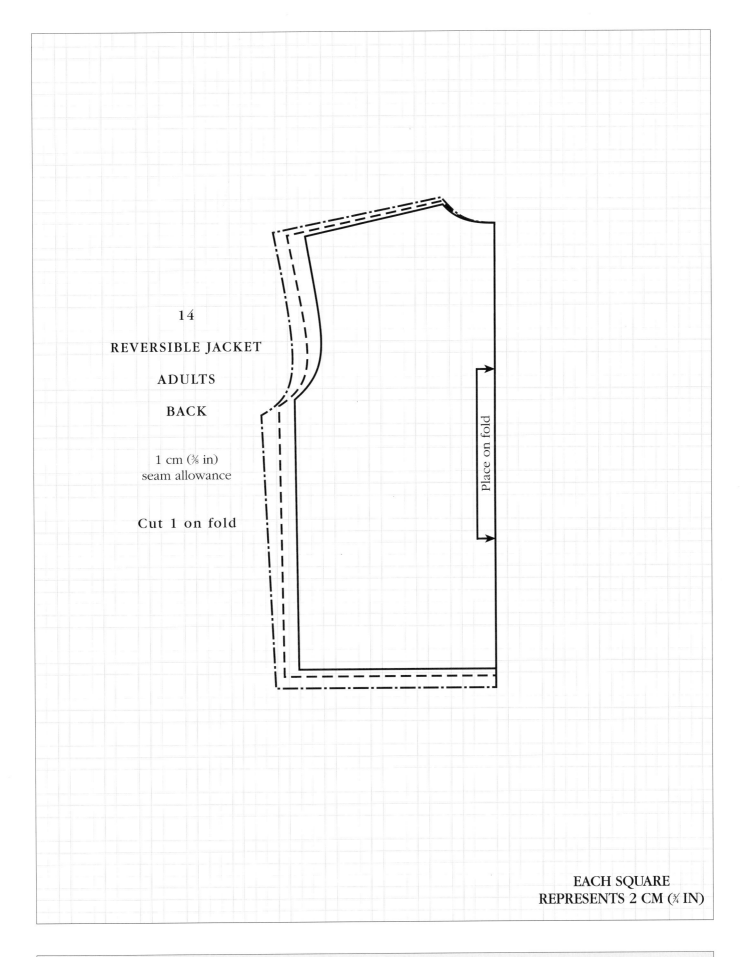

14

REVERSIBLE JACKET

ADULTS

BACK

1 cm (⅜ in)
seam allowance

Cut 1 on fold

Place on fold

**EACH SQUARE
REPRESENTS 2 CM (¾ IN)**

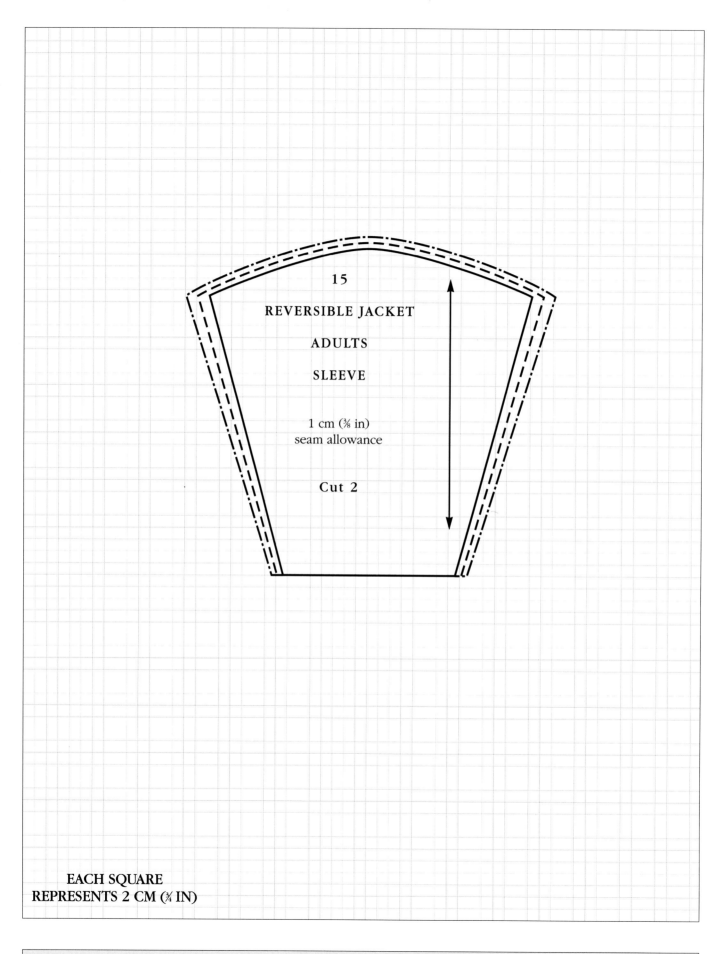

15

REVERSIBLE JACKET

ADULTS

SLEEVE

1 cm (⅜ in)
seam allowance

Cut 2

**EACH SQUARE
REPRESENTS 2 CM (¾ IN)**

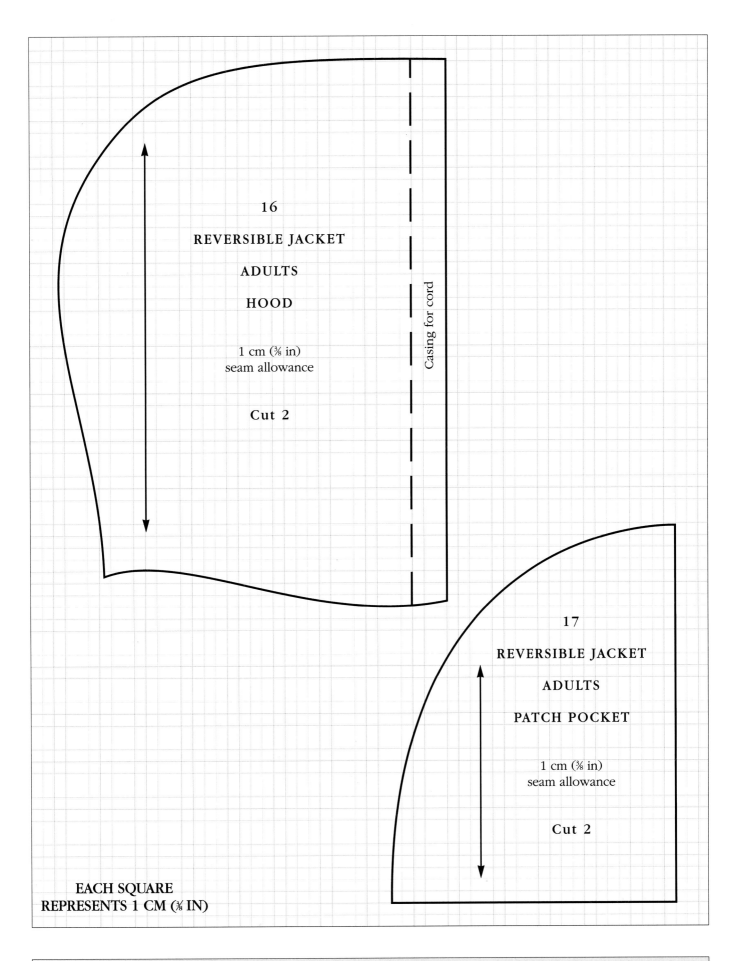

16

REVERSIBLE JACKET

ADULTS

HOOD

1 cm (⅜ in)
seam allowance

Cut 2

Casing for cord

17

REVERSIBLE JACKET

ADULTS

PATCH POCKET

1 cm (⅜ in)
seam allowance

Cut 2

**EACH SQUARE
REPRESENTS 1 CM (⅜ IN)**

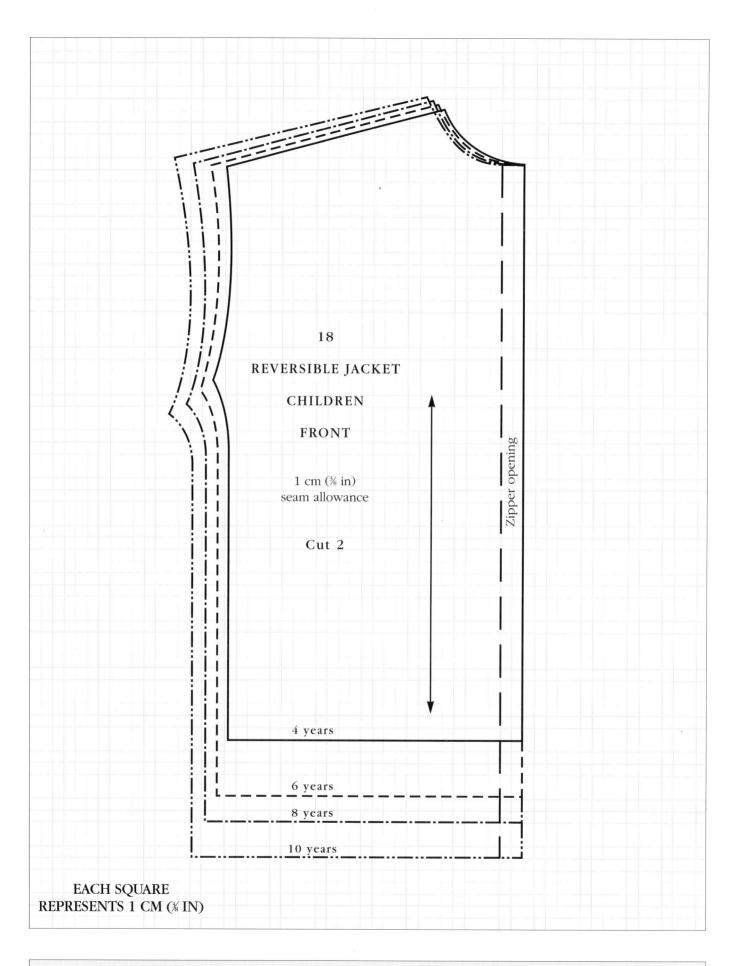

18

REVERSIBLE JACKET

CHILDREN

FRONT

1 cm (⅜ in)
seam allowance

Cut 2

Zipper opening

4 years

6 years

8 years

10 years

**EACH SQUARE
REPRESENTS 1 CM (⅜ IN)**

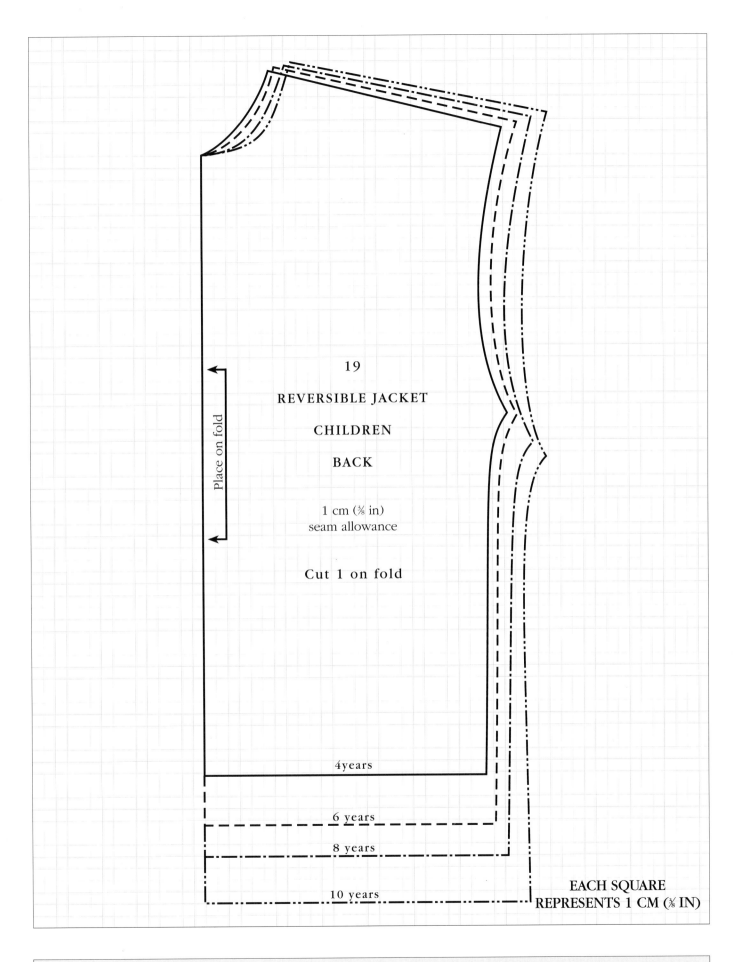

19

REVERSIBLE JACKET

CHILDREN

BACK

1 cm (⅜ in)
seam allowance

Cut 1 on fold

Place on fold

4years

6 years

8 years

10 years

EACH SQUARE
REPRESENTS 1 CM (⅜ IN)

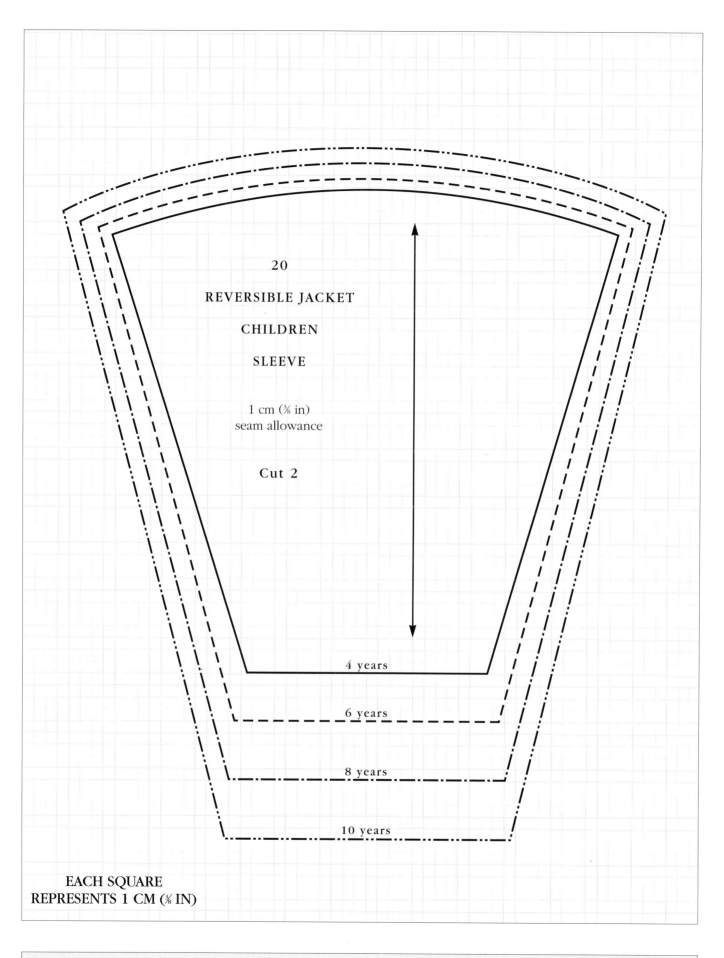

20

REVERSIBLE JACKET

CHILDREN

SLEEVE

1 cm (⅜ in)
seam allowance

Cut 2

4 years

6 years

8 years

10 years

EACH SQUARE
REPRESENTS 1 CM (⅜ IN)

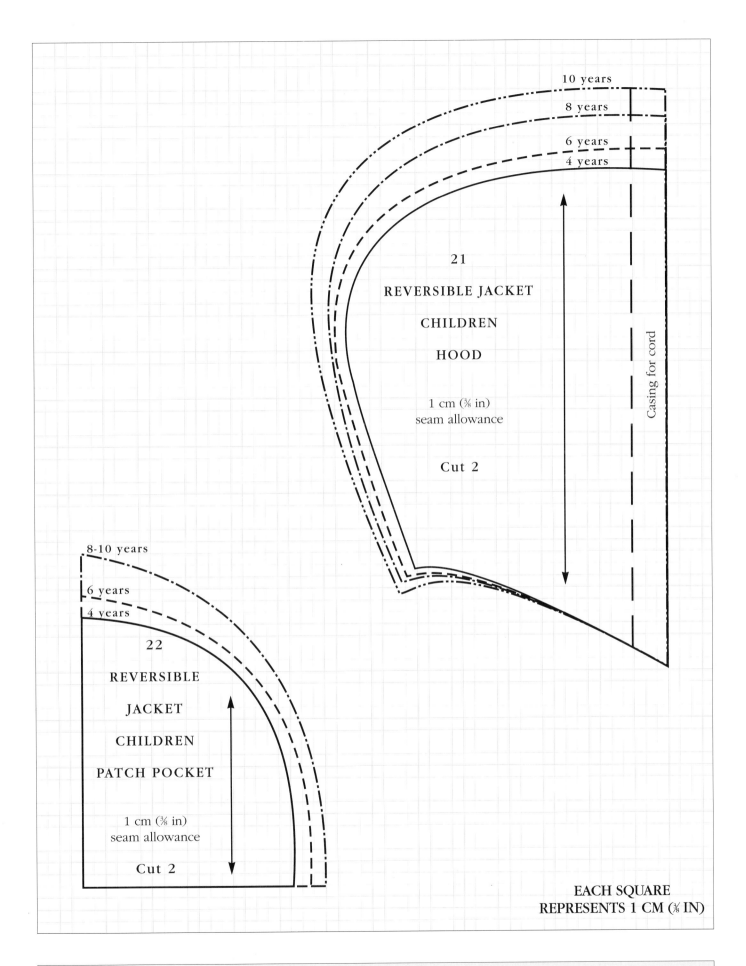

10 years

8 years

6 years

4 years

21

REVERSIBLE JACKET

CHILDREN

HOOD

1 cm (⅜ in)
seam allowance

Cut 2

Casing for cord

8-10 years

6 years

4 years

22

REVERSIBLE

JACKET

CHILDREN

PATCH POCKET

1 cm (⅜ in)
seam allowance

Cut 2

**EACH SQUARE
REPRESENTS 1 CM (⅜ IN)**

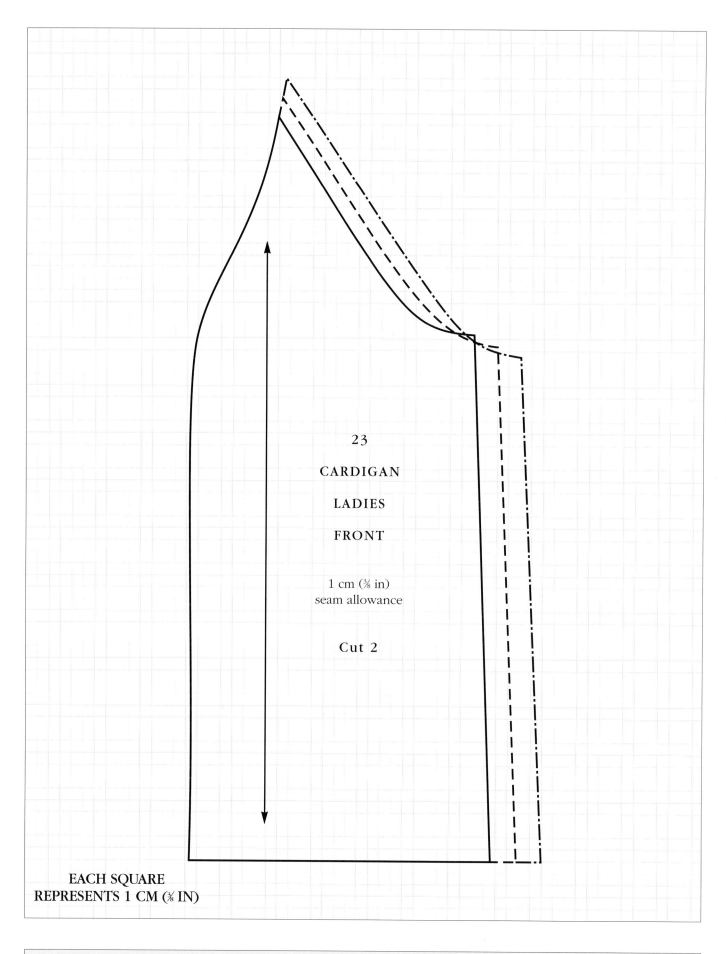

23

CARDIGAN

LADIES

FRONT

1 cm (⅜ in)
seam allowance

Cut 2

EACH SQUARE
REPRESENTS 1 CM (⅜ IN)

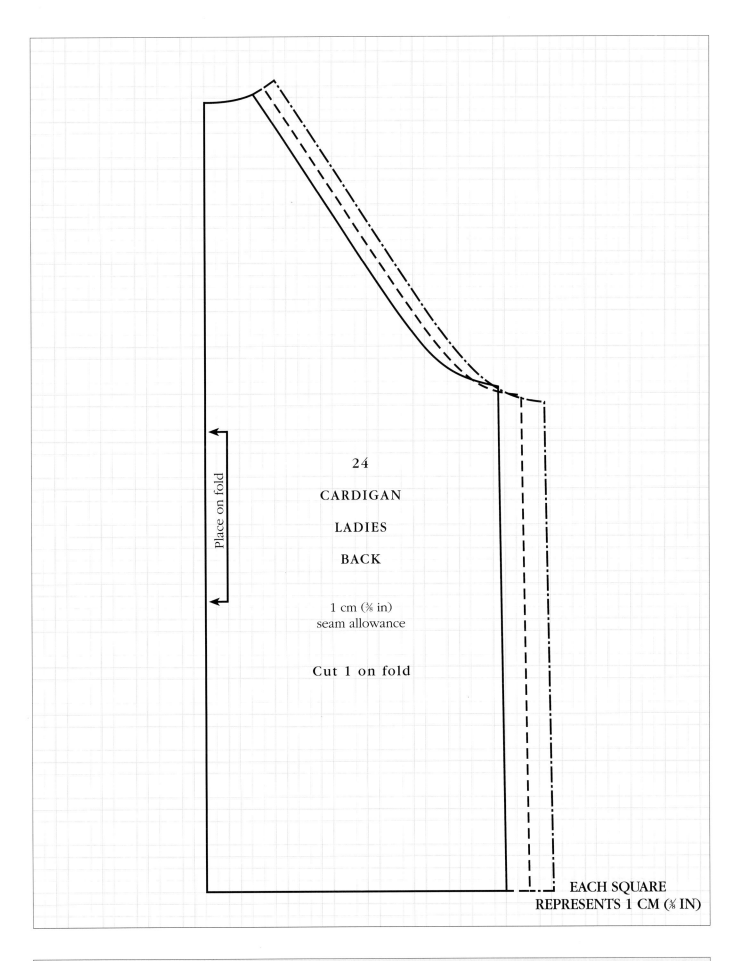

Place on fold

24

CARDIGAN

LADIES

BACK

1 cm (⅜ in)
seam allowance

Cut 1 on fold

EACH SQUARE
REPRESENTS 1 CM (⅜ IN)

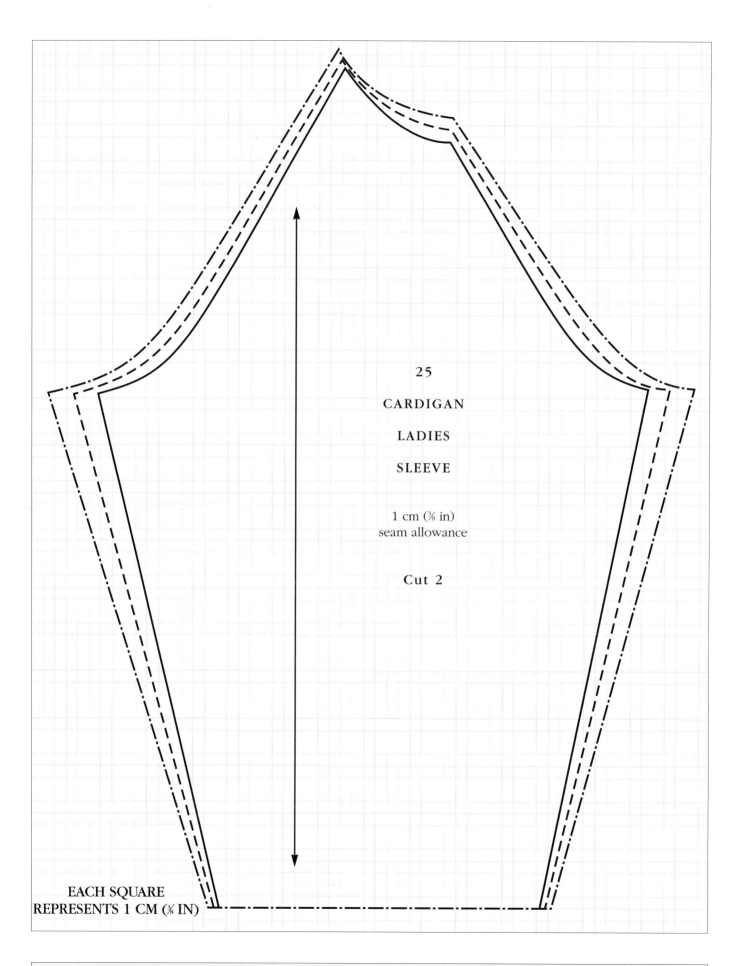

25

CARDIGAN

LADIES

SLEEVE

1 cm (⅜ in)
seam allowance

Cut 2

EACH SQUARE
REPRESENTS 1 CM (⅜ IN)

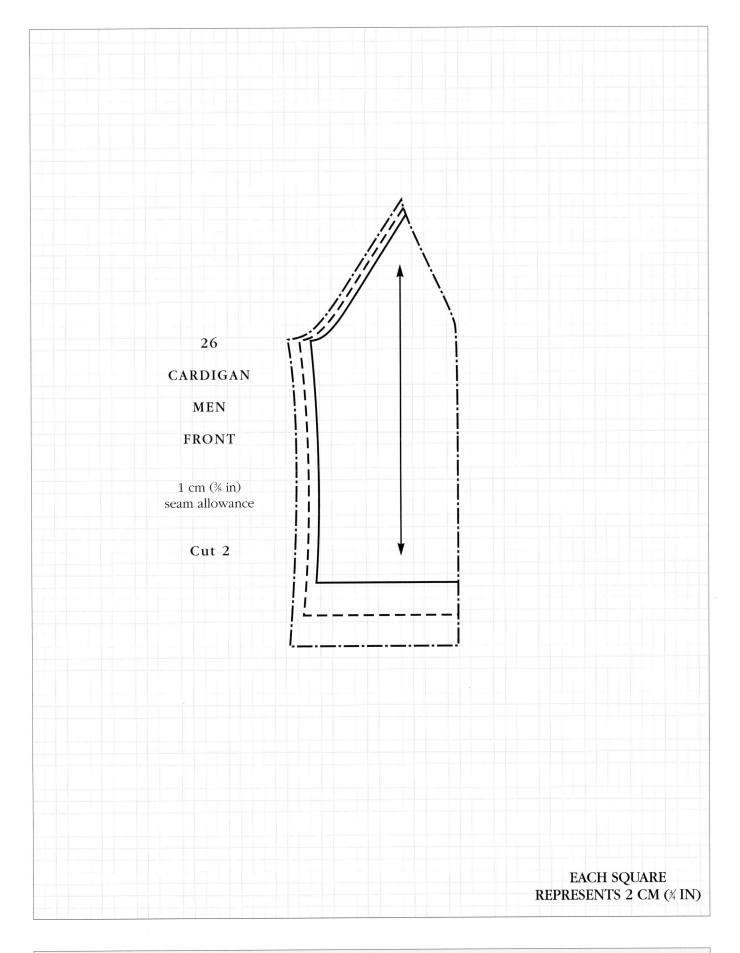

26

CARDIGAN

MEN

FRONT

1 cm (⅜ in)
seam allowance

Cut 2

EACH SQUARE
REPRESENTS 2 CM (¾ IN)

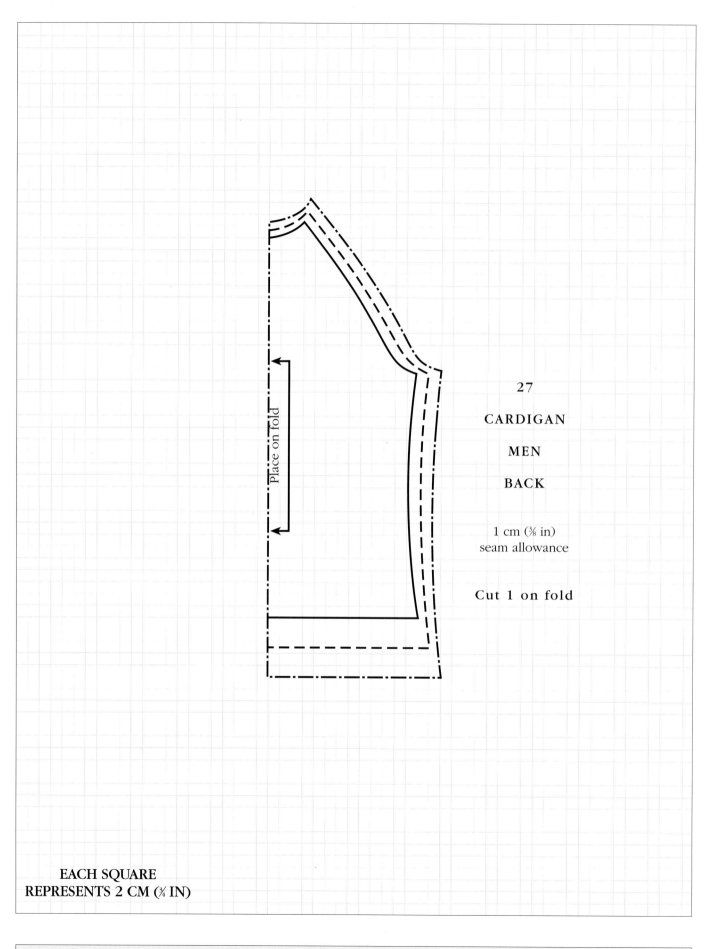

Place on fold

27

CARDIGAN

MEN

BACK

1 cm (⅜ in)
seam allowance

Cut 1 on fold

**EACH SQUARE
REPRESENTS 2 CM (¾ IN)**

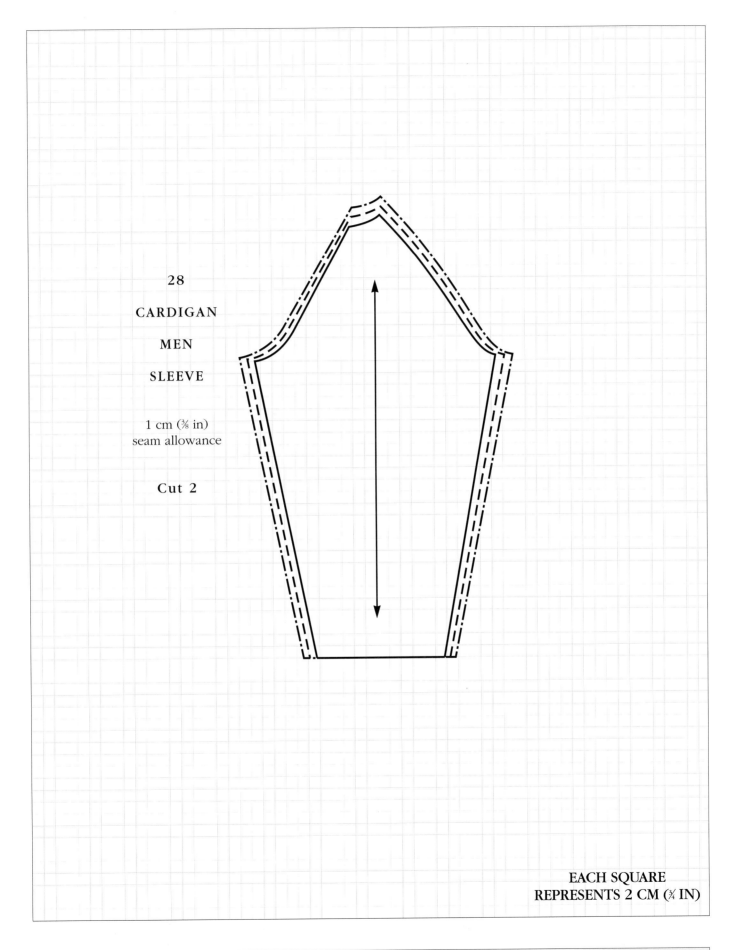

28

CARDIGAN

MEN

SLEEVE

1 cm (⅜ in)
seam allowance

Cut 2

**EACH SQUARE
REPRESENTS 2 CM (¾ IN)**

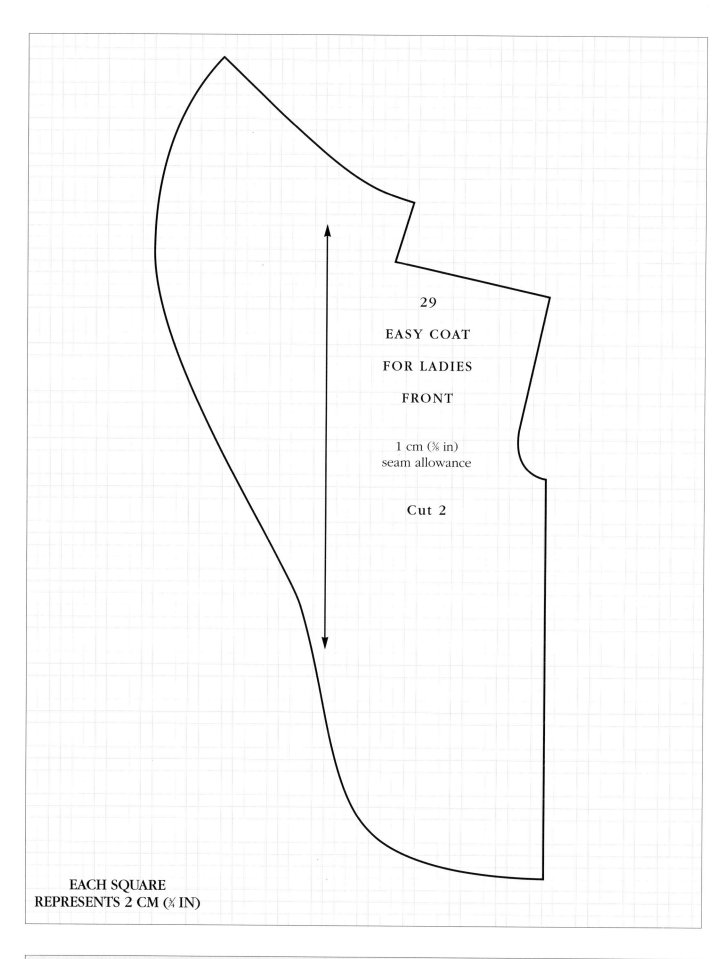

29

EASY COAT

FOR LADIES

FRONT

1 cm (⅜ in)
seam allowance

Cut 2

EACH SQUARE
REPRESENTS 2 CM (¾ IN)

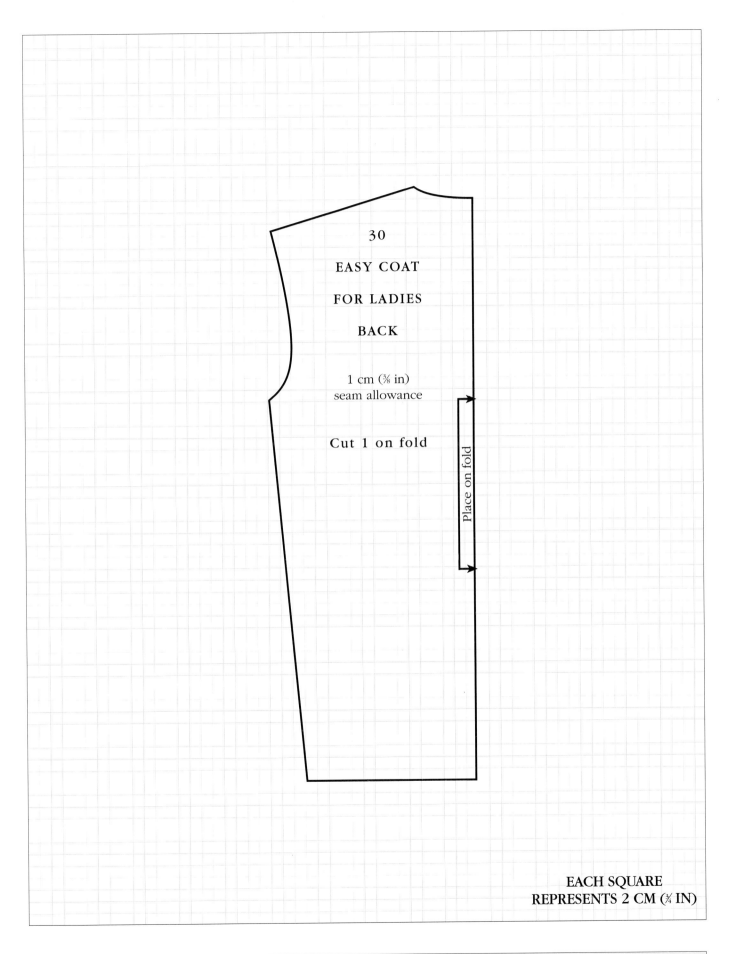

30

EASY COAT

FOR LADIES

BACK

1 cm (⅜ in)
seam allowance

Cut 1 on fold

Place on fold

**EACH SQUARE
REPRESENTS 2 CM (¾ IN)**

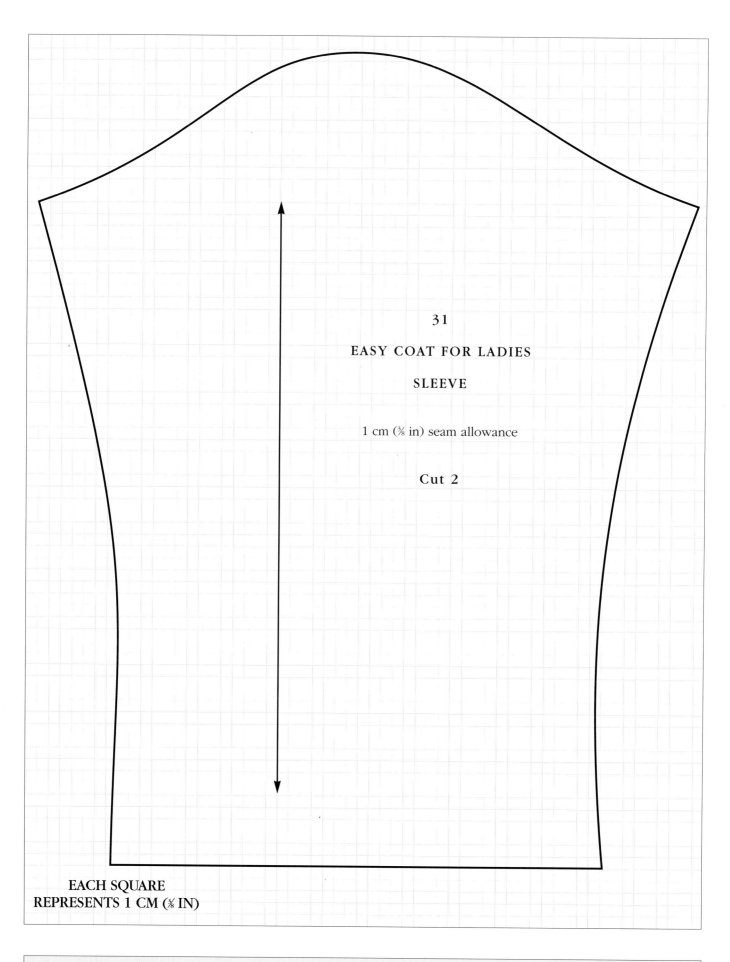

31

EASY COAT FOR LADIES

SLEEVE

1 cm (⅜ in) seam allowance

Cut 2

**EACH SQUARE
REPRESENTS 1 CM (⅜ IN)**

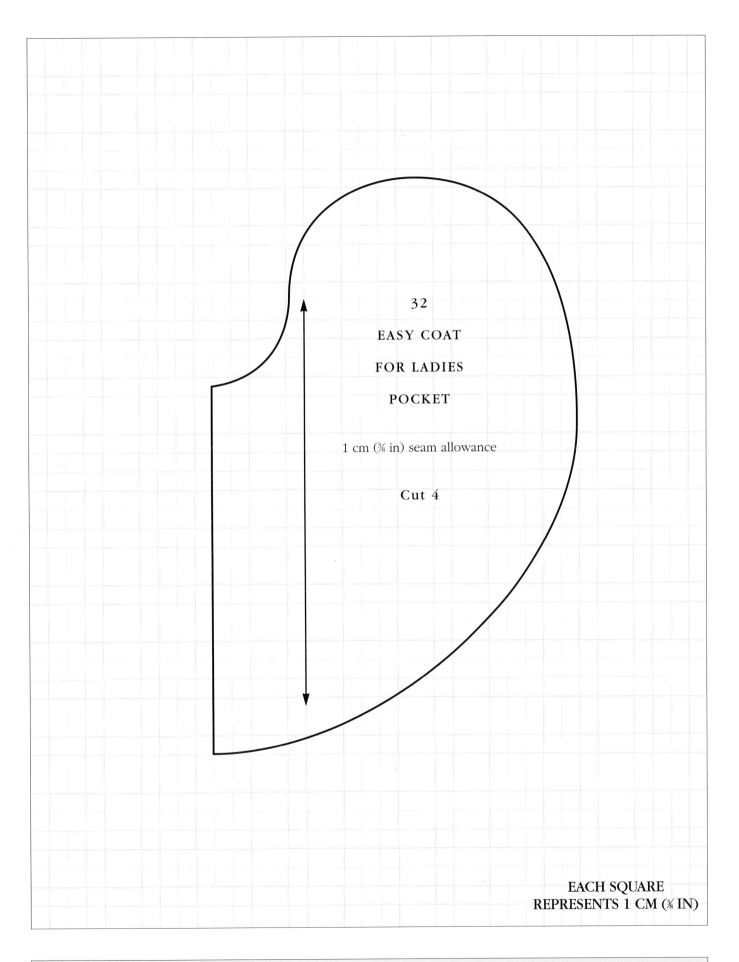

32

EASY COAT

FOR LADIES

POCKET

1 cm (⅜ in) seam allowance

Cut 4

**EACH SQUARE
REPRESENTS 1 CM (⅜ IN)**

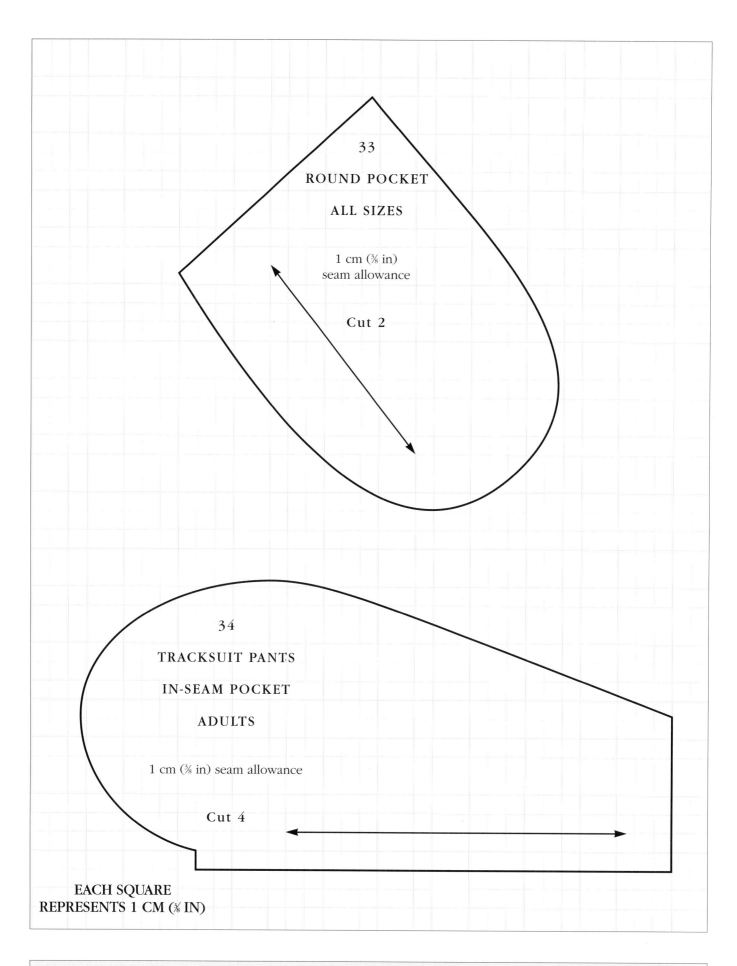

33

ROUND POCKET

ALL SIZES

1 cm (⅜ in)
seam allowance

Cut 2

34

TRACKSUIT PANTS

IN-SEAM POCKET

ADULTS

1 cm (⅜ in) seam allowance

Cut 4

EACH SQUARE
REPRESENTS 1 CM (⅜ IN)

SUPPLIERS' ADDRESSES

UNITED KINGDOM

For local suppliers please consult the Yellow Pages under Fabric Retailers
(fabrics, haberdashery) or Sewing Machines Domestic.

JOHN LEWIS PARTNERSHIP
278-306 Oxford Street
London W1A 1EX
0171-629 7711

LIBERTY PLC
Regent Street
London W1R 6AH
0171-734 1234

BOROVICK FABRICS LTD
16 Berwick Street
London W1V 3RG
0171-437 2180

ELNA SEWING MACHINES (GB) LTD
39 Southwark Bridge
London SE1 1AA
0171-403 3011

BERNINA SEWING MACHINES
Bogood House
50 Great Sutton Street
London EC1V 0DJ
0171-253 1198

JONES & BROTHER
Shepley Street
Audenshaw
Manchester M34 5JD
0161-330 6531

**NEW HOME SEWING
MACHINE CO LTD**
Janome Sewing Machine Co
(Europe) Ltd
Cromwell Road
Bredbury
Stockport SK6 2SH
0161-430 6011

PFAFF BRITAIN LTD
Pfaff House
East Street
Leeds LS9 8EH
01533 760330

NEW ZEALAND

BERNINA SEWING CENTRE
St Lukes Shopping Centre
St Lukes Square
Auckland
Tel: (09) 849 4610

**JANOME SEWING MACHINE AND
OVERLOCKER SPECIALISTS**
336 Remuera Road
Remuera
Auckland 5
Tel: (09) 520 0496

Also at:
Lynmall City
Great North Road
New Lynn
Auckland
Tel: (09) 827 7043

AUSTRALIA

**A.A. ALL APPLIANCE
RENTALS PTY LTD**
146 Liverpool Road
Enfield NSW 2170
Tel: (02) 744 3838

BERNINA AUSTRALIA
15 Carrington Road
Castle Hill NSW 2154
Tel: (02) 899 1188

PFAFF
Head Office
Unit 1, 13 Hoyle Avenue
Castle Hill NSW 2154
Tel: (02) 894 6311
(outlets also located in
most suburbs)

**OVERLOCKER ADVICE
SERVICE & SALES**
20 Memorial Avenue
Liverpool NSW 2170
Tel: (02) 602 8144

OVERLOCKERS GALORE
325 Belmore Road
Riverwood NSW 2210
Tel: (02) 534 1690

Also at:
53065 Westfield Shopping Plaza
Miranda NSW 2228
Tel: (02) 540 2578